MOUNTAIN BIKE GUIDE

Mountain Bike Guide County Durham

by

DEREK PURDY

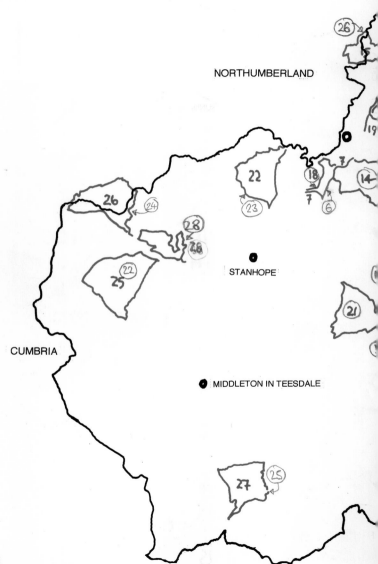

NORTHUMBERLAND

CUMBRIA

STANHOPE

MIDDLETON IN TEESDALE

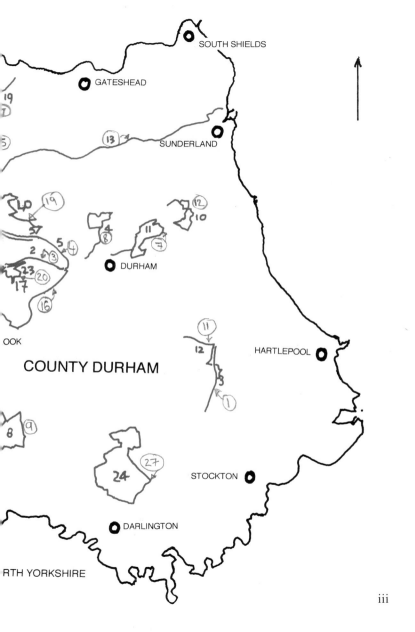

SOUTH SHIELDS

GATESHEAD

SUNDERLAND

DURHAM

HARTLEPOOL

COUNTY DURHAM

OOK

STOCKTON

DARLINGTON

RTH YORKSHIRE

iii

CONTENTS

ACKNOWLEDGEMENTS

It would be a lonely job riding all the routes for a mountain bike guide by yourself, although it must be said that in the case of County Durham it would be highly unusual if you didn't meet someone along the way. Not often cyclists, but the traditional pursuit of the pitman, despite the demise of his collieries, lives on. You will find folk walking between villages through the fields, along the now defunct railway lines, but they did this when they were working, and it will be a rare day if you don't have a horse or two peering over a wall or wandering across a paddock to see you. Thanks to all these passing acquaintances. In addition, there have been more deliberate companions, both on the official route checking rides and over the past few years on days of exploration, some successful, some near total disaster! Rob Aynsley came along to prove the standard for the younger riders, and vanished into the distance, Suzy Rutter impressed both her dad, Jeff and the author whilst what are probably the youngest riding companions a cycling writer ever had, Jill Mary and Paul Martin Wonders, seven and a quarter and five and a half years respectively, proved excellent and entertaining companions on the shortest route in the book, Rowlands Gill to Hamsterley Mill. Jeff Rutter also endured some of the harder days out; Alex Spence, with his local knowledge of the Willington area provided valuable support on some bleak days of early exploration; and Malcolm Williams who laughed too loudly when the author sank up to his thighs near Chopwell Woods, wasn't allowed to come again! That particular route is not in the guide! Thanks are also due to the Rights of Way Department of Durham County Council, in particular to Jo Futter who has supplied a steady stream of advice. Finally, wife Pam, who washed muddy gear, was occasional chauffeuse and even fell off a couple of times just to prove she was there.

1

INTRODUCTION

THE COUNTY

County Durham might not be the biggest in England, but it is one of the most diverse. People outside the county often labour under the misapprehension that it is all coal mines and heavy industry, but this was never true. Sadly the collieries and the steelworks are gone, but even when they hummed at their most industrious there were always fields, valleys and often moors within walking distance. You will find evidence of mines and quarries everywhere you go, from the very edge of the North Sea to the highest hills of the Pennines, but likewise you will find greenery everywhere and many pockets of truly outstanding beauty.

The routes in the guide have been split into three main categories. Railway routes, either wholly or partly over dismantled railways that have been converted into linear parks, although like the mines, it is difficult to avoid the myriad of lines that criss-crossed the county, even if the ride doesn't deliberately fall into this category. The second group lie mainly near the coast and are best described as village hopping rides, utilising roads, lanes, bridleways and inevitably an old railway or two that interconnect the old mining communities. Lastly there are the rural rides, forays out into the magnificent wilder parts of the county, traversing, on separate routes the two highest public through roads in England, Harthope Head and Killhope Cross. Could your cycling be complete without these under your belt?

The biggest group are the railway rides, and Durham County Council must be congratulated on their tremendous foresight in adopting and converting the old railways for leisure use. They are foremost in the country.

RIGHTS OF WAY

There is no right of way for bikes along a public footpath, unless you have permission from the landowner. Cyclists do have a right of way along bridleways provided they give way to pedestrians and horses, and of course on tracks of higher status e.g. byways and public roads. There is an ongoing commitment by local authorities with regard to Roads Used as a Public Path (RUPPs) to reclassify them as either footpaths, bridleways or byways open to all traffic (BOATs). Most will probably end up as bridleways, although there are vehicular rights along many, so you should be safe to use them on a bike.

You will soon discover that there is a tremendous variation in the standard of bridleways in particular, many actually being roads with loose surfaces, but some being merely a line drawn on the map with next to nothing on the ground.

MAPS

Despite their shortcomings, Ordnance Survey maps are still the best available. Each ride has a sketch map, but this is intended as a visual synopsis of the route, no more. Please plot your intended route on the appropriate 1:50,000 OS Landranger map using the information from the "Plotting Plan" and carry it with you. It is essential that you have the proper map in case you need to escape from the route due to fatigue, injury or mechanical breakdown. You will need five Landranger maps to cover the entire county. They are:

87 Hexham, Haltwhistle & surrounding area
88 Tyneside & Durham area
91 Appleby-in-Westmorland area
92 Barnard Castle & surrounding area
93 Middlesbrough & Darlington area

The 1:25,000 Pathfinder maps show more detail, although you would need 22 of them, and just to cause confusion many are being superseded by the new Explorer series, others in upper Teesdale already having been swamped by Outdoor Leisure map number 31.

Plotting a map reference

All Ordnance Survey maps have a grid of squares superimposed upon them. The sides of the squares are exactly one kilometre, or 1000 metres, regardless of the scale of the map. The Landranger series are produced to the 1:50,000 scale, the Pathfinder, Outdoor

Leisure and Explorer series are all 1:25,000 but still have the one kilometre squares. Every Landranger map has an individual number as well as a name e.g. "Landranger 92 Barnard Castle & surrounding area", and also a letter reference relating to the British National Grid. We do not need the letter reference. Our main concern, as far as this guide goes, is the need to identify specific, local locations in order to transfer the information given in the plotting plan onto the OS map, by means of a six figure reference, which will place the spot in a 100 metre square. Details of how to plot such a reference are given in the key on every Landranger map.

Map references in this guide are given either as: "Hamsterley village green 92/115311", which means you will find Hamsterley village green on Landranger 92, at map reference 115311, or as simply "Doctor's Gate 070329". The latter, which appears more often will be found in the Plotting Plan list after the map has been identified, in this case 92. If the route spills over from one Landranger map to another, as in the case of "Waskerley Way for Sprogs", the map change will be notified with the first relevant reference.

In some cases the map reference is deliberately slightly "off" to ensure the correct track is taken.

SAFETY & EQUIPMENT

Buy a good, fashionable crash helmet and wear it. There is no choice, you must protect your head. Glasses come a close second, they keep mud, dust and vegetation out of your eyes. Even if you normally wear spectacles a bit extra protection doesn't come amiss. I have a pair of Bolle Edge 2 shades with my prescription glasses mounted behind, made by Sports Specs of Manchester. Cool, trendy even, but supremely practical.

If you are not already a first aider, the time spent on a first-aid course could well reap rewards for the rest of your life. First-aid kits can get right out of hand if you try to cater for every eventuality, but a small kit, such as those that can be bought at Boot's for about £1.00, containing plasters, gauze, a couple of antiseptic wipes, a large piece of sticking plaster and a pair of scissors, augmented by a small tube of antiseptic cream, which might double as emergency lubrication should a chain fail! are worth carrying at all times. It's amazing what a dab of antiseptic cream can fix.

A mountain biker, acting as a courier, can seek help far faster than any pedestrian, but don't get carried away, literally. Becoming a casualty of over enthusiasm, particularly on the downhills, will not help at all!

Always carry personal identification, particularly when travelling alone, it will save the rescue services a lot of time if the worst happens. Last items are a whistle, compass and the skill to use it, a Poly bag or Survival Blanket, and coins for the "Please collect me I'm knackered" phone call. You should be self sufficient for both yourself and your bike every time you venture out onto the hill.

CLOTHING

Your enjoyment of mountain biking will be greatly enhanced if you invest in proper padded cycling shorts or liners from the outset. Synthetic chamois needs no maintenance other than regular washing and dries quite quickly.

Proper mountain bike shoes or boots are also preferable. The stiffer soles transmit more power to the pedals than trainers, but don't buy very stiff-soled racing shoes because in cross-country mountain biking there are many occasions when you will be forced to walk. Boots and gaiters are the equipment of the hard men who refuse to let rain and snow keep them in the house, but the sound of the gaiters catching every turn of the crank will either drive you mad or bring total reassurance.

You can get away with just about anything in summer, but for most of the year the northern climate can give you anything from sub-tropical to Arctic on any day. Clothing must be comfortable and functional. Calange, Karrimor, North Cape and Polaris all produce excellent clothing specifically designed for the mountain biker. You will soon realise that a system of layers is best in this high energy sport, so try to build up a wardrobe containing a good wicking base layer which will conduct the sweat away from your body, a good warm mid layer that will provide comfort and warmth in most situations, and a windproof shell that will keep you warm on long descents, or in cold winter conditions. You can beef up any of the mid or outer layers for winter, but don't be tempted to go for a completely waterproof shell – you'll probably drown in your own sweat! Total breathability is paramount.

THE BIKE

Bike preparation is also paramount. You are supposed to be going out riding and enjoying the countryside, not attempting to remedy mechanical failure in an inhospitable environment. Bits can break at any time, but first class maintenance and inspection pays dividends. Even if you are not a mechanical genius you can keep your bike clean and well lubricated, so do that at least.

There are one or two tweaks that add to comfort. Make sure your saddle has a sealed surface so water doesn't get in and squelch about with every turn of the pedal, the same applies to handlebar grips. When fitting new tyres or fixing a flat give them and the inner tube a good dressing of talcum powder, a 70 pence tin of Apple Blossom from Superdrug will last for years – just don't let anyone see you buying it! Some sort of mud protection is also well worthwhile. I came off Edmundbyers Common the other day in conditions of melting snow with everything working flat out, the Crud Catcher taking the worst of the water off the front wheel, the Race Guard doing great service at the back and the little Crud Claw scooping out snow and mud from the back block . . . and my legs were still saturated. Perhaps I shouldn't have been out at all, but I'm sure you get the drift. Every little bit helps.

Your toolkit will reflect your confidence in your preparation, but there is a minimum. A selection of suitable Allen keys, small adjustable wrench which will double as a spoke key, one tyre lever, piece of soft wire (1001 uses), pair of mini pliers, especially for the winter when fingers can be numb, spare tube which will get you moving quickest and keep you warm, puncture repair kit in case you get more than one puncture, pump, or even a gas cartridge which will inflate the tyre instantly, although a pump will inflate an infinite number of tubes. Wrap everything, except the pump, in a rag which will go into your saddle pack under the seat along with the mini first-aid kit, tube, survival blanket and in my case, even a Polaris Pertex jacket.

Lights and reflectors are required if you ride on a public road after dark, and you never know when you may be caught out, especially in the short days of winter.

ROUTE GRADING

The gradings are an attempt to convey the difficulty of the route, taking into consideration the overall distance of the ride, which is an obvious factor, technical difficulty which is largely impossible to assess from the map, the amount of map reading and route finding involved, and the exposure factor, or in some cases the pure wildness. Technicality rates more difficulty, so you will find short rides with high grades.

Obviously the weather can have a great bearing on any route, and may well have had on my impression on the day, but I have tried to take this into consideration. Low level rides can tolerate quite large variations in weather and still be enjoyable, but high level rides can turn really nasty when wind, rain, snow or even hot weather prevail. Don't take chances. Get off the hill if the weather is too bad, you can always go back in better conditions, and probably enjoy it a lot more.

FOOD AND SHELTER

There is little in the way of food on most of the rides, although most villages have a pub, and most pubs do bar meals or snacks, some very good indeed! Part of the enjoyment, for me at least, is dining al fresco with the enjoyment of the views, the surroundings, and often the inquisitive wildlife. I still recall with great pleasure sitting against a dry-stone wall high in the Pennines and being joined by a cheeky stoat, popping his head out between the blocks as he worked his way ever closer, eventually refusing my cheese. Snob! Carry a picnic, it will bring all sorts of rewards.

Get out of the wind whenever you stop. You will cool naturally after the effort you've been putting in, but if there is any wind at all you may well chill. Get behind a wall, shed, or even in a hollow, and put your coat on, unless of course it is one of those staggeringly beautiful summer days when you'll actually take your shirt off to dry it in the sun.

SKETCHMAP SYMBOLS

Tarmac road

Other tarmac road

Track or unsurfaced road

Other track or unsurfaced road

Well-defined bridleway

The rides along dismantled railways are shown as bridleways apart from the Consett & Sunderland route, which is shown as a continuous line.

Other well-defined bridleway

Poorly defined bridleway or single-track

Buildings

Church or chapel

Bridge

Trees

River or stream

Working railway

The former Thorpe Thewes station, now the Visitors´ Centre.

Winter riding on the northern half of Caslte Eden Walkway.

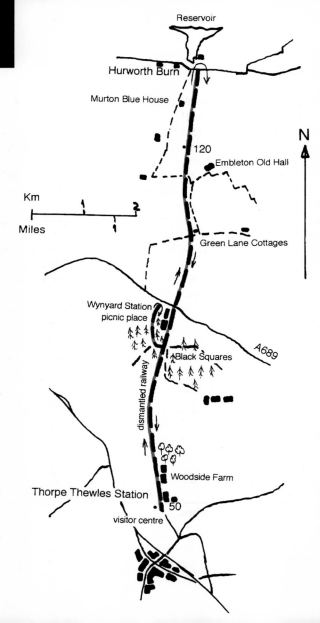

1. CASTLE EDEN WALKWAY

Grade:	1/2. 1 to Wynyard Station, 2 to Hurworth Burn, 3 if it is wet!
Total distance:	8.6 km (5.3 miles) to Wynyard Station picnic place and return, 18.7 km (11.6 miles) to Hurworth Burn and return
High point:	120 m, 1.1 km south of Hurworth Burn railway bridge, so it is gently uphill on the outward journey, and downhill on the way back.
Map:	OS Landranger 93 Middlesbrough & Darlington
Facilities:	Refreshments (summer only) and toilets at the Walkway Visitor Centre, Thorpe Thewles Railway Station, otherwise this is a picnic ride, and by far the best way to appreciate your surroundings on a good day.
Note:	Cyclists must give way to pedestrians, especially on the southern half of the Walkway, and stick to the track – keep out of Thorpe Wood.

PLOTTING PLAN	App.	Map ref.	Dep
START: Thorpe Thewles Station (Woodside Farm)	-	93/402244	N
Black Squares crossing or turn left (W) to Wynyard Station picnic place at 401283 for short route	SSW	402277	NNE
A689, care when crossing	SSW	405284	NNE
Green Lane Cottages	S	408299	N
Hurworth Burn railway bridge. Northern limit	S	409332	S
Turn around and retrace to Thorpe Thewles at	N	402244	-

The Castle Eden Walkway follows the track of the Castle Eden Branch Line, closed in 1966, which carried coal from the Durham coalfield to Middlesbrough, where it was either used as fuel in the iron and steel industry, or exported. The line was laid down in the 1870s, but like many others, passenger traffic ceased in the 1930s as motor transport became the preferred form of transport.

It is hoped that the current stretch from Thorpe Thewles to Hurworth Burn will eventually be extended northwards and possibly linked to the coast, and that at the southern end funds will be made available for a link to Stockton.

Railway embankments were always havens for bird life. I can recall men attempting to trap linnets for breeding when I was a boy, by luring them into specially built cages, and a linnet was one of the first birds we saw as we pedalled north from the old railway station which acts as the information centre. You will see blackbirds, chaffinches, blue tits, great tits, goldfinches, wrens, and as winter visitors we came across a huge flock of fieldfares ploating[1] the berries. There will be no shortage of entertainment.

In addition to the birds the Walkway is one of the top sites in the area for butterflies, no doubt due to the careful management of the trackside bushes and trees, and the careful preservation of a large variety of herbage. For much of its length the line-side drainage ditches remain, ideal spots for toads, newts and frogs, as they always were. I wonder if there are sticklebacks in any of the larger pools?

THE RIDE

Walk onto the station platform, north through the self-closing gate, then simply follow the track as far as you like, or right up to Hurworth Burn. The first couple of kilometres is good firm path, dressed with dolomite but quite narrow so remember the courtesy of giving way to pedestrians.

Don't be alarmed by the notice on the gate, that you will see facing you on your return, saying "This section of the walkway is not a bridleway". We asked the countryside ranger, who told us it is OK for bikes as long as you give way to walkers.

[1] Ploat – pluck

North of the gate the surface is looser and more likely to hold water, so expect to splash through a few puddles. There is also a little section over a bridge that can be quite muddy and need more control and effort, although it will be totally dry at the height of summer.

Two gates close together in coniferous forestry and blue bridleway arrows mark the point where you can deviate around to the Wynyard Station picnic place. If this is as far as you are going, and it's quite a good idea if there are children in the party, turn left and follow the forest road until you arrive at the benches.

Immediately north of these gates the track is grassy and bumpy, but it only lasts as far as the A689 dual carriageway. Care crossing this very busy road, then follow the farm road parallel to the old railway for 200 metres, when you will be able to jink left through a barrier back onto the railway. The farm road is a fine example of one of the countryside rights of way anomalies you will encounter quite frequently. The track to the farm is obviously a road, used by tractors and all kinds of motor vehicles, but it is only legally a footpath and therefore not available to bikes, unless, as has happened for the first 200 metres, there is a special agreement with the landowner. You can't judge the status of a thoroughfare by what you find on the ground.

Once you rejoin the old line you simply follow it all the way to Hurworth Burn railway bridge, another 4.9 km (3.1 miles) farther on. The surface varies from narrow single track weaving between the old railway hedges, to long stretches of ash, punctuated by little dips and climbs where the old bridges have been removed. Much of it is elevated, giving you great views of the surrounding countryside. Why not ride all the way to Hurworth Burn keeping an eye out for a good picnic spot, turn around having completed the outward leg, then ride back a little way and enjoy your trackside bait[2]. You've done all the hard work, it's downhill from here.

[2] Bait – sandwiches

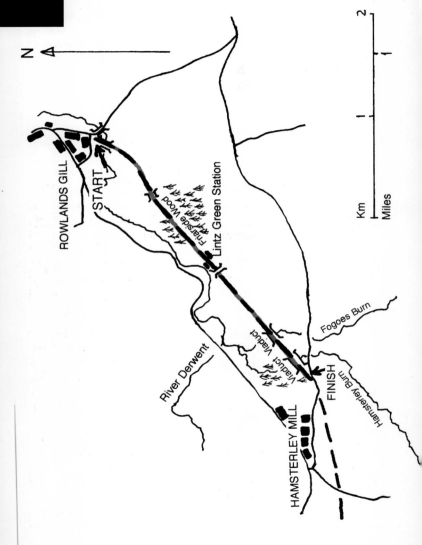

ROWLANDS GILL

START

Frolicside Wood

Lintz Green Station

Viaduct Viaduct

River Derwent

Fogoes Burn

HAMSTERLEY MILL

FINISH

Hamsterley Burn

N

Km

Miles

2

1

1

2. DERWENT WALK FOR BAIRNS

Rowlands Gill to Hamsterley Mill Viaduct

Grade:	1
Total distance:	6.6 km (4.1 miles)
High point:	Hamsterley Mill Viaduct, high in more ways than one!
Map:	OS Landranger 88 Tyneside & Durham area
Facilities:	Fish & chips in Rowlands Gill. Picnics are best.

PLOTTING PLAN	App.	Map ref.	Dep.
START: Stirling Lane carpark, Rowlands Gill	-	88/167581	SW
Lintz Green station	NE	150567	SW
Hamsterley Mill Viaduct, turn around, retrace to Rowlands Gill	NE	145562	NE

Virtually any stretch of any of the railway walks in County Durham are suitable for children of any age, but I chose this section of the Derwent Valley Walk, from Rowlands Gill to Hamsterley Mill viaduct because it is totally traffic free, no road crossings at all, and full of interest for the youngest rider. Some of the interest, in the shape of the huge high viaducts at Lintz Green and Hamsterley Mill is quite dramatic, and the children loved it!

The riders were Paul and Jill Wonders, five and a half and seven years respectively. We walked up from the carpark onto the railway, which turned out to be a bridge with a concrete deck, full of immediate interest with Paul peering through the railings and announcing he could see a pond. The fact that it was the River Derwent took a little explaining, especially in view of the fact that only a short stretch of the river could be seen due to tree cover. We

15

both compromised and agreed that "even if it is a river it looks like a pond!"

I wondered how they would fare on the long straight uphill through Friarside wood. This stretch between Rowlands Gill and Lintz Green was the only double width when the line was working and the gentle but unrelenting grade is set in a deep, wide cutting for most of its length, and must look enormous to a five-year-old, but no fear, there are big blocks of stone to contemplate, clear running water, a couple of lineside ponds to investigate and ultimately an overbridge where echoes can be tested. The latter was so successful, I wondered whether it had been a good idea to suggest it, especially when Paul did a big shout on the return journey which obviously alarmed a pair of walkers!

Jill likes horses and was suitably impressed by the paddocks and the ponies at Lintz Green station. There was a long break at the old station itself with investigation of the platform, the access steps, one still boasting two excellent iron gates, a crossing of the bridge to come down the steps onto the other platform, and of course another echo session under the bridge.

The final section was the short run from Lintz Green station to its splendid viaduct, which spans the Fogoes Burn, then another two hundred metres farther on the impressive Hamsterley Mill viaduct which spans the Hamsterley Burn. Jill insisted on taking pictures down onto the treetops and across the valley to the rooftops of Hamsterley Mill. Needless to say there were the usual gory discussions on the consequences of a fall, or as Paul suggested, a dive from the bridge, but the visit went off without incident.

We returned to Lintz Green station for the picnic, then it was downhill all the way back to Rowlands Gill. Having declared he was tired, and inquired when the picnic was taking place about four times on the outward journey, there was a query free return by Paul, who must have covered at least another kilometre more that the rest of us with his weaving course, testing every centimetre of the track . . . and a fair amount of the vegetation too! "When are we going again Derek?"

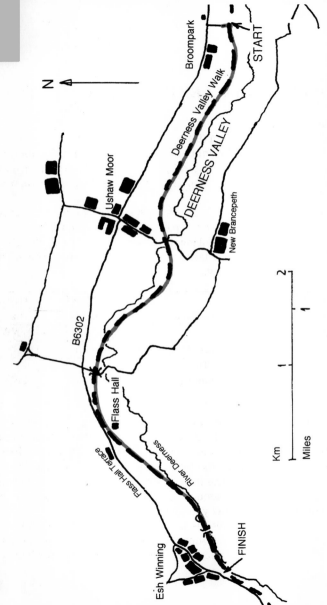

3. DEERNESS VALLEY FOR BAIRNS

Grade: 1

Total distance: 15.3 km (9.5 miles) All off-road

High point: Esh Winning 130 m, but this is not really relevant, the route starting at 85 m above sea level and the climb virtually unnoticeable on the railway gradient.

Maps: OS Landranger 88 Tyneside & Durham area – whole ride shown as part of Deerness Valley Walk

Facilities: Nothing at the start, but pub grub, fish & chip shop, Chinese take-away and ice cream available in Esh Winning.

PLOTTING PLAN	App.	Map ref.	Dep.
START: Broompark Picnic Area	-	88/251415	W
Deerness Valley Walk	ESE	233420	WNW
Deerness Valley Walk, Flass Hall	NE	204426	SW
Esh Winning picnic area. Turn around and retrace to Broompark Picnic Area	ENE	191416	ENE

In reality this isn't only a route for the bairns, it is a supreme introduction to off-road riding for anyone, but of course being completely traffic free is eminently suitable for children. Fifteen kilometres may well be too far for some youngsters, especially if weather conditions are less than perfect, but there is no need to press on to Esh Winning. Turn around and retrace whenever the need arises. A picnic lunch will allow you total flexibility.

The old trackway now has a smooth surface and is mostly well drained, although in wet winter weather there can be a few long pools to add to the excitement. If there are repercussions when you arrive home with offspring splashed by black water, blame me! This is a route you can use at any time of year. Ideal for first rides with a new bike after Christmas, excellent for seeing the birds at their most active in spring, incredible for the range of flowers you will encounter throughout summer, and when the autumn leaves fall you will be stunned by the variety. It might sound as if you should carry the Shell Guide to the Birds of Britain and a copy of Collins Wild Flowers, but they might help you to answer some of the harder questions you may well be asked *en route*!

Suzy Rutter and her Dad accompanied me on the official traverse of the route in January, but I have been back several times since then – it is one of those open-ended journeys where you can press on beyond the book description, or simply have a flash along for an hour after work, or even put the lights on and use it in the dark winter nights. Quite brilliant.

BROOMPARK to ESH WINNING

A small brown forest-walk sign points you into the Broompark picnic area off the B6302. Park on the concrete then make your way across the grassed area to the direction boards, where you turn right (west) with the Deerness Valley Walk. Don't be confused by the sign for Ushaw Moor which you pass on our ride, and for some reason is signed in the opposite direction.

Railway embankments were always havens for wildlife in their working days and these continue in the same vein. The display varies throughout the year, but at the end of summer you will see the tall purple rosebay willowherb, bright yellow golden rod, hawksbeard and common toadflax, which look like miniature antirrhinum, white yarrow and clover, and of course blackberries and rowan berries hanging in surprisingly large bunches on surprisingly small trees.

After 2.8 km (1.7 miles) you cross the road that connects Ushaw Moor and New Brancepeth, preceded by a pair of motorcycle barriers. The view is limited, so take care in crossing to, and through the Ushaw Moor carpark. Giant rhubarb flanks the river here and you swap sides without noticing as you ride, or more likely walk the path at the far side. The old wooden bridge survived here until the 1960s, but now it's a bit of an effort to regain railway height. The pit heap at the top was planted with rough conifers many years ago, despite grave doubts from the local sages that "nowt'll grow on there": but they were wrong, there is now quite a little forest on the left, flanking the track. Opposite the pines there is a small pond, best seen in winter or spring when there are few leaves on the trees, often frequented by an old heron.

Farther along I met a man out with his six-year-old son trailing behind, looking rather red and tired, his coat neither off nor on. We exchanged greetings, but the last thing I heard was "Dad, can I have a bike?" Obviously wheeled transport held much more attraction than walking.

Another bridge is missing when you recross the river, which by now is no more than a large stream, but the far hill is loose and sustained, demanding a bit of effort. A kilometre farther on you cross the private road to Flass Hall and enter more open countryside. This is the best stretch for birds in spring, the number of great tits being most impressive. Across the fields on the right you will see a row of houses, Flass Hall Terrace – nothing unusual in the fact that they are white brick in these parts, but this is real quality, every block being a perfect rectangle to engineering standards. Most impressive.

In the final couple of kilometres the railroad weaves over concrete bridges which can be inundated by the spring thaw or winter floods; there is a very leafy section through mature woodland, then you reach Esh Winning. There are benches around the edge of the little playing field and the main street is only metres away should you require substantial refreshment.

Esh Winning is a tidy village and well worth riding through if all the party have good road sense. Newhouse Roman Catholic school again built of white brick, but not to Flass Hall Terrace standard, is impressive for a community of this size and there are many well kept excellent long narrow gardens, typical of a pit village. You can rejoin the railway by using another old spur at the end of the houses or more easily at Flass Hall.

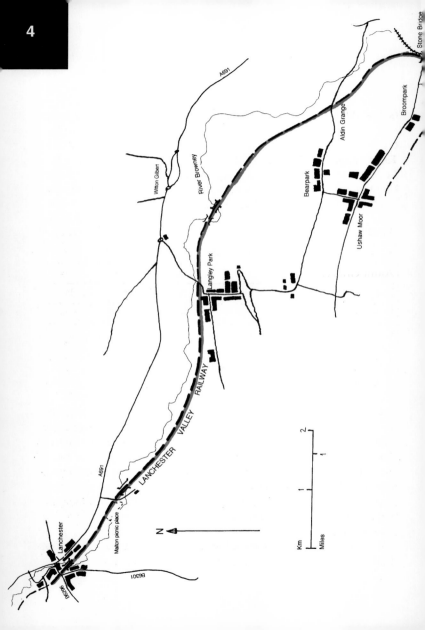

4

4. LANCHESTER VALLEY RAILWAY

Grade: 2
Total distance: 25.6 km (15.9 miles)
Map: OS 88 Tyneside & Durham area
Facilities: Stone Bridge Hotel a short distance from the start,
                 several pubs in Lanchester

PLOTTING PLAN	App.	Map ref.	Dep.
START: Stone Bridge, Broompark	-	88/251415	E
Aldin Grange	SE	246429	NW
Langley Park	E	205451	W
Lanchester, B6296	SE	165473	NW
End of outbound route. Refresh, turn around.	SE	163475	SE
Return to Stone Bridge using the outbound route.	E	275472	S

This is a railway ride that is still maturing. When I first rode the route in 1993 the huge Broompark pit heap had recently been roughly landscaped and was still a mountain of shale and colliery debris. There was a sea of windblown plastic decorating the perimeter fence and adjacent trees, but by the summer of 1996 there were mountain bikers camping on the eastern slopes. I don't know whether this was a tribute to the efforts of the planners or the lunacy of mountain bikers, but there is now a good covering of tough grass and trackside trees actually bearing fruit.

    We took along a young friend, Rob Aynsley, to demonstrate that this is a family ride, but the rascal set off at a tremendous pace and maintained it all the way to Lanchester. There were sly attempts to slow him down by sporadic interest in the industrial archeology of the line, mainly in the shape of splendid girder bridges, but once rolling again he pressed on regardless, refuelled from the extensive bait box his mother had prepared, then did the same on the way back. Fortunately we played a blinder by stopping to pick some most excellent blackberries near Langley Park, whereupon he fell into a ditch and subsequently slowed to our pace! Sorry Rob, but you did look good with only a helmeted head poking out of the rosebay willowherb!

The railway follows the valley of the River Browney, a short but major tributary of the River Wear. It starts 91 metres above sea level and only climbs 29 metres in the 12 kilometres (7.5 miles) to Lanchester. Anyone can cope with that. Much of the track is very open, affording great views of the surrounding countryside, but inevitably there are extensive wooded sections, rich in wildlife as one would expect alongside an old railway.

If you have a "Rob" with you there are a couple of minor diversions to maintain interest and sap strength in the shape of little paths parallel to the track between the Malton Picnic Place and Langley Park. They aren't easy to see, but if you poke your front wheel over the low embankment on the south side of the track you'll find a technical little path weaving its way through the birches. Mind your head on the lowest branches, you will immediately realise the benefit of glasses and helmet.

This is a route to enjoy. You needn't ride all the way to Lanchester if someone starts to run out of puff. Stop, investigate the flora and fauna, take your time with your picnic, and dawdle back. And if some young fellow on a red Giant mountain bike passes you with head down, going like a train, it's OK, it's only Rob.

Setting off through the stone bridge at Broompark, Route 4.

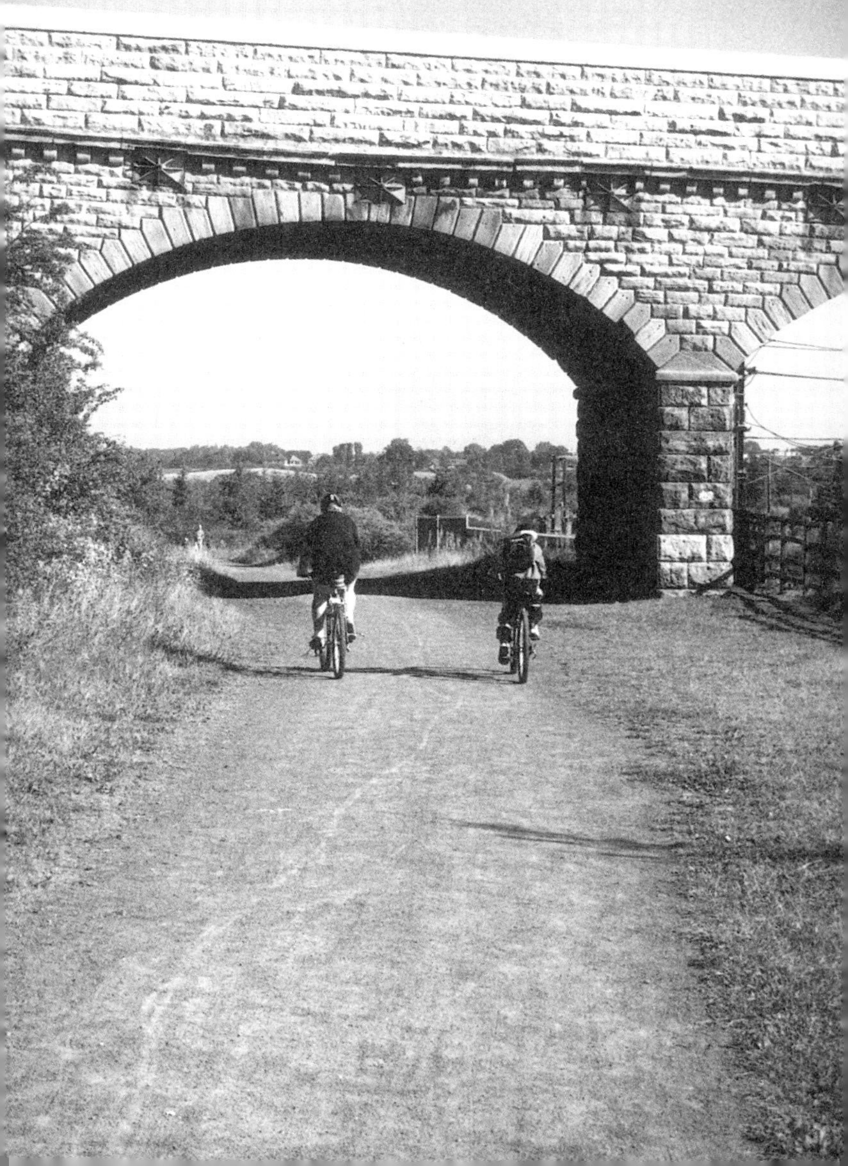

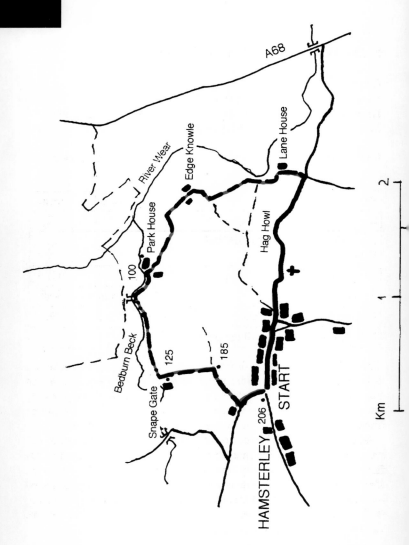

A68

River Wear

Edge Knowle

Lane House

Park House

Hag Howl

100

Bedburn Beck

125

185

Snape Gate

206

HAMSTERLEY

START

Km

2

1

5. HAMSTERLEY BACK LANES

Grade: 3
Total distance: 6.5 km (4.0 miles)
High point: The start, Hamsterley village green, 206 m
Map: OS Landranger 92 Barnard Castle & surrounding area
Facilities: Cross Keys for pub grub, and public toilets in Hamsterley

PLOTTING PLAN	App.	Map ref.	Dep.
START: Hamsterley village green	-	92/115311	E
Lane House crossroads. SP Park House Farm.	NW	134308	N
Park House bridge	ESE	123321	WSW
Snape Gate	ENE	116320	SSE
Unclassified county road	NE	114313	SE
FINISH: Hamsterley village green	NW	115311	-

This ride flies in the face of what I usually preach, that all mountain bike rides should finish with a wacky downhill if at all possible. In this case the downhill comes right at the start, down the road you probably came along to Hamsterley village, losing nearly 100 m in height in the first two kilometres, but you've got 76 kph (47.2 mph) to beat!

We seriously considered routing this the other way around, but came to the conclusion that novice riders might be tempted by its lack of length, mistakenly thinking it might be easy, but it is not. The climb from Snape Gate is a killer, very steep, liberally sprinkled with tree roots, muddy sections and the occasional loose stone. Try it the other way 'round, down through this lot, but only if you are totally competent in the technical department.

THE RIDE

Ride east through the village, past the Cross Keys and down the winding hill that rejoices in the title Hag Howl. Please do not alarm other road users with the obvious sound effects! After two kilometres turn left towards Park House Farm at the signposted crossroads, onto rougher stuff.

The route now follows what is obviously the main farm track, all the way to Park House. You weave past Lane House farm, then turn right, still with the main track, at the white gate. (White gate! Jeff saw my note and burst out laughing. All the gates are white, but you'll see what I mean when you get there.) Turn left at Edge Knowle, spelled Knoll on the map, then weave your way through excellent valley floor farmland to Park House.

The bridleway lies down the side of the farmhouse, through another white gate. Do not use the "Private Road" – the bridleway is more fun anyway, slithering down to the bank of the Bedburn Beck then left, upstream until you rejoin the main farm road again. The road now follows the beck around to the private Park House bridge, but we stick to our side, hugging the river bank and following the trees along to a black(!) gate The track immediately thereafter is splendid, a most pleasant run along through the riverside trees until you are confronted with another non-white gate. Hug the fence on the right, across to Snape Gate where you turn left up the steep technical hill.

Even at the height of summer this is a cruel challenge. On the winter day when the single track was covered in leaves which hid many of the roots and several nasty little sticky sections, neither of us managed farther than the gnarled tree close to the wall. It's like a trials course, only 520 metres long! A black mink shot into the dry-stone wall only twenty metres ahead of us, there were deer droppings and huge rabbits in the top field. Keep your eyes peeled.

When you reach the very top of the hill, turn right after the wicket gate and ride what is fast becoming single track along to the unclassified road which will take you back into the village. We thoroughly enjoyed it, and finished in time to dodge the black snow clouds that were sweeping down Weardale.

The excellent bridleway above Bedburn Beck toward Snape Gate, Route 5

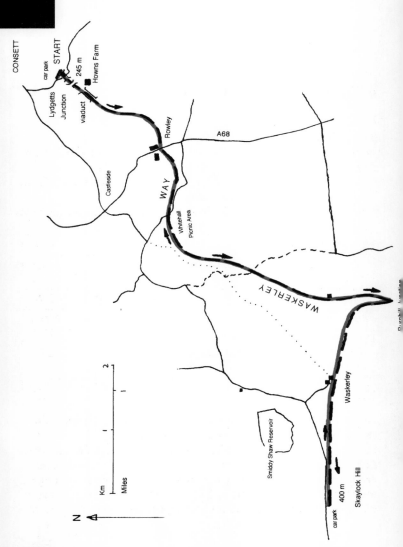

CONSETT

car park
Lydgetts Junction
START
viaduct
245 m
Howns Farm
Rowley
A68
Castleside
W A Y
Whitehall Picnic Area
WASKERLEY
Durehill Junction
Smiddy Shaw Reservoir
Waskerley
Skaylock Hill
400 m
car park

N

Km
Miles

2
1

6. WASKERLEY WAY FOR SPROGS

Grade:	3
Total distance:	22.2 km (13.8 miles). All off-road
High point:	Skaylock Hill 400 m, end of the outbound route
Maps:	OS Landranger 88 Tyneside & Durham area
	OS Landranger 87 Hexham, Haltwhistle & surrounding area
Facilities:	Full facilities in Consett, nothing at all on the route

PLOTTING PLAN	App	Map ref	Dep
START: Lydgetts Junction, near Howns Farm, Consett	-	88/100494	SW
Rowley, A68, care	ENE	087479	SW
Burnhill Junction	NNE	87/064444	NNW
Skaylock Hill carpark. End of outbound ride, turn around and retrace Waskerley Way to Consett.	E	032453	E
FINISH: Lydgetts Junction	SW	88/100494	-

Apart from two road crossings this route is totally off-road, entirely on the old line that has become the Waskerley Way. Unfortunately the ride currently ends at the Skaylock Hill carpark, but if it is restored to its former grandeur there will be another four splendid kilometres around and above Waskerley Reservoir. We live in hope. If younger members of the party start to lose momentum there is no need to complete the ride, you can turn back at any time that suits you. My young partner, Rob Aynsley, only started to run out of puff on the way back which is virtually all downhill, through pressing on at an impressive speed!

Consett stands well above the Derwent Valley, the start of the ride is 245 m above sea level and the route climbs to 400 at Skaylock Hill. In summer this is a pleasant airy ride, but in winter, especially in windy conditions it is exposed and not the place for youngsters. Having said this we have had some splendid days along the old line, crunching through frozen snow with only the grouse and the occasional inquisitive sheep for company.

There are limited opportunities to create loops which include the old line, but all involve substantial climbs and descents as soon as you leave the railway (one is included later in the guide) but this is the easiest way to the heights.

CONSETT to ROWLEY

The area immediately west of Consett is in a state of redevelopment, but if you head towards Castleside you should have little difficulty in locating the start. It is marked by one of the slag hoppers from the defunct Consett Iron Works perched atop the old railway that has become the Waskerley Way.

Sustrans had a hand in the creation of this route and there are many examples of their innovative recycling of railway paraphernalia, particularly in the first few miles. The first is a cycle tunnel which leads through a leafy cutting and bang, out onto the super impressive Howns Gill viaduct, built in 1858, fifty metres above the valley floor.

When the line was first opened there was a system of cradles and steam-powered lifts to carry the little trucks of limestone, lead and iron down and up the sides of the valley; then later funicular railways on either side taking three trucks at a time. The final, and most effective solution was the building of the viaduct by the railway's third owners, the Stockton & Darlington Railway Company. If you keep a sharp look out you will still see some of the famous S & D R milestones out on the moor beyond Waskerley.

The route shrinks to single track at the far end of the viaduct. There is still the full line width available but everyone seems to use one narrow path – it all adds to the fun. This situation persists all the way to Rowley Station with added interest in the shape of wild raspberries in summer.

Rowley Station isn't there anymore, you'll find it as one of the main features of the Beamish Open Air Museum, and should you ever find yourself in the town of Langholm, in the Borders, you can see the signal switching display on the wall in the cafe. Take care when crossing the A68 road.

ROWLEY to WASKERLEY

By now you are committed to the route. More single track takes you around to the Whitehall Picnic area, where the gradient bites a bit; then the countryside takes on a more open aspect as you climb to Burnhill Junction. The Way turns sharp right at Burnhill, along the side of an old arms depot where the trees planted to disguise the place have now reached maturity, then heads NNW to Waskerley itself. We once rode across to the woods from Waskerley on a route-finding exercise only to be amazed when confronted by a huge steel gate in the middle of the moor which once gave access to the depot.

Only the old engine shed and a couple of farm buildings now remain at Waskerley, where once there had been a goods station, sidings, a shed for six engines and wagon repair shops. When the line closed in 1968, the railway village, which had boasted houses for the railway men and their families, a church, chapel, school, and shops, became a ghost town, and now the fields and moors are claiming the countryside back. The final leg up to the carpark, where you will see metre square blocks which were the original railway sleepers, might reveal one of those S & D R milestones. Then it is about turn and back the way you came, but nearly all downhill. There is an old quarry which will provide shelter for your picnic, and possibly a red grouse that will cry "back, back back!" just to remind you.

Rob Aynsley and the old slag hopper at the start of the
Waskerley Way, Route 6.

One of the ancient Stockton and Darlington milestones
near Waskerley.

Rob heading up Round Hill toward Red House Farm.
One of the more exposed stretches of Route 6.

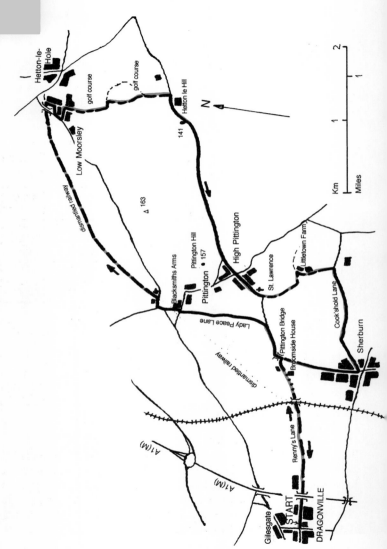

Hetton-le-Hole

golf course

golf course

Hetton le Hill

141

Low Moorsley

dismantled railway

△ 163

N

Pittington Hill
• 157

Pittington

High Pittington

Blacksmiths Arms

St. Lawrence

Littletown Farm

Lady Peace Lane

Cook'sholl Lane

Sherburn

dismantled railway

Pittington Bridge

Broomside House

Renny's Lane

A1(M)

A1(M)

Gilesgate

START

DRAGONVILLE

Km

Miles

2   1   1   1

36

7. DRAGONVILLE AND PITTINGTON

Grade: 3
Total distance: 19.9 km (12.35 miles)
High point: Hetton le Hill, 141 m
Map: OS Landranger 88 Tyneside & Durham area
Facilities: Several pubs on the route, including the Gilesgate Moor Hotel which is the start and finish point.

PLOTTING PLAN	App.	Map ref.	Dep.
START: Gilesgate Moor Hotel, Dragonville	-	88/297428	E
Pittington Bridge	WSW	320433	NE
Join dismantled railway	W	325452	NNE
Hetton le Hole, quit railway	WSW	348470	SW
Golf course track	N	352460	S
Hetton le Hill	NE	350452	SW
St. Lawrence church	N	328436	SE
Cook'shold Lane	ENE	327426	W
Pittington Bridge	S	320433	WSW
FINISH: Gilesgate Moor Hotel, Dragonville	E	297428	-

This route typifies Durham for me. It contains several little tracks, all of which get walked and cycled, not just by mountain bikes but by anything with wheels, regardless of their legal status. Pitmen always walked or cycled through the fields between villages, and although the pits have passed, the habits remain, and not only remain, but are given fresh life by a new generation.

There are very few signposts on this ride, so on one hand it might be a test of your navigational skills, but on the other it has added spice as you weave your way around the district.

Durham is wick[6] with old railways and this route is no exception – you will ride along them, under them, and be tempted to stray by lines that scream out to be investigated, so hopefully this ride will open the door to further adventure.

I would have liked to have given an explanation for the name Dragonville, but alas my research has come to nought. However, Gilesgate village spans one of the oldest thoroughfares emanating from Durham City and provides one of the best views, the parish church standing higher than the cathedral. One can only wonder how the bishops allowed it!

GILESGATE MOOR to HETTON LE HILL

Obviously you can ride out from Durham City to Dragonville, but there is room to park at the trading estate if you arrive by car, and the Dragonville Trading Estate is signposted from the A1(M) and other directions.

Depart east from the Gilesgate Moor Hotel along Renny's Lane, signposted "No Through Road" and "Karting Centre". The estate road shrinks as you swoop under the A1(M), then becomes even narrower as you pass behind the houses, soon developing a distinct single-track feel as you weave through the lineside vegetation. This is further enhanced as you drop down to a small bridge then climb up to the rail tunnel north of Sherburn.

Immediately on exiting the tunnel, the route lies straight ahead up the side of a field, towards Broomside House farm, the lesser of three options, only two of which are shown on the map. This rough bridleway improves considerably to a farm road, as you crest the hill, then all you do is follow it down to the unclassified road at Pittington Bridge.

Turn left and follow the road, missing a right turn, all the way to the crossroads at the Blacksmiths Arms. This is Lady Peace Lane, shown on OS maps as Lady's Piece Lane but this is incorrect. It

[6] Wick – wicked

takes its name from the murder of Mary Ann Westropp who was cruelly murdered on 8 August 1830 at nearby Hallgarth Mill, allegedly by her lover who was executed at Durham on 28 February 1831. Her ghost is said to walk this road and her cries are heard as far away as High Pittington, but none claim to have seen her.

Straight on at the crossroads, then first right after 340 metres and look for a tiny slot between the houses on the left that will lead you through to another old railway. There is a fading pink (I think) arrow saying "Wearside Walks" and a motorcycle barrier giving confirmation. This is limestone country, you will see bits of creamy coloured stone and bricks of the same hue in the black track, and high on the hill the old quarries of Pittington and Moorsley. The lineside is abundant with roses and a fine selection of trees but up on Pittington Hill you will find wild strawberry, violets, thyme, hairbell and cowslips. Yet another temptation!

Quit the railway at the first brick overbridge you encounter, after 2.5 km (1.55 miles) on the outskirts of Hetton le Hole, weave right to join the road you have just passed under, turn left towards Moorsley, then left again into Nidderdale Road after 200 metres, past the shops then first right towards a row of garages (painted red in 1996). Ride around the garages and across the field behind them to a motorcycle barrier, then straight up the side of the golf course. Stick with the "dolomite" track fringing the golf course for 870 metres after the barrier, then turn right up the side of a field just after the dolomite track makes a ninety degree turn left. Black posts and a small motorcycle barrier mark the spot. You rejoin the dolomite track up the side of the golf course after about 300 metres and climb to the unclassified road where you turn right for home. The top of the rise is Hetton le Hill, the highest point on the route.

HETTON LE HILL to DRAGONVILLE

The road is mainly downhill to High Pittington crossroads, where you go straight across then turn left towards St. Lawrence church. The Rev. Arthur Shepherd, vicar of Pittington, who died in 1770 had a hatchet with him in the coffin and a glass plate in the lid opposite his face "with a view to facilitate his resurrection" according to the historian Surtees. He was then buried, presumably in a shallow grave, in the churchyard with the same thing in mind.

An excellent little bridleway now wends its way down behind the church and through the fields to Littletown Farm, where you turn right through a black wicket gate bearing a fading "Bridleway" in white, to join the farm road which takes you to the unclassified Cook'shold Lane, which in turn leads to Sherburn, once famous for its lazar-house or lepers´ hospital.

When you reach the T-junction in Sherburn, turn right, then a kilometre later at Pittington Bridge, turn left onto the track we used on the outbound leg and retrace all the way to Gilesgate Moor. The climb from the little bridge back up Renny's Lane comes as a bit of a sting in the tail, especially if it is as windy as the day of my reconnaissance ride when I was showered with crab apples near the A1(M) underpass!

Now a confession! I had intended to continue south from Littletown as far as Shadforth, then use the bridleway north from Running Waters back to Sherburn; but became well and truly saturated between Hetton le Hole and Pittington. By the time I reached Cook'shold Lane, I was shivering and feeling quite rough, so curtailed the ride. But there's nothing to prevent YOU doing it all!

The railway path near Pittington weaving its way
through ancient spoil heaps, Route 7.

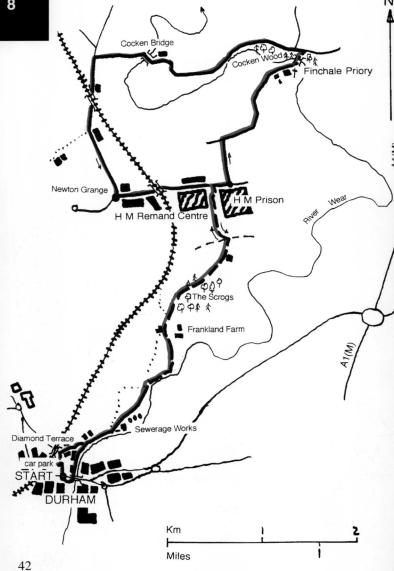

N

Cocken Bridge

Cocken Wood

Finchale Priory

A1(M)

River Wear

Newton Grange

H M Prison

H M Remand Centre

The Scrogs

Frankland Farm

A1(M)

Diamond Terrace

car park

START

DURHAM

Sewerage Works

Km

Miles

8. DURHAM TO FINCHALE PRIORY

The godly and the godless!

Grade: 1
Total distance: 17.6 km (10.9 miles). Off-road constituent: Loose
                        tracks and hard-packed single track 4.8 km (2.95
                        miles). Tarmac: 12.8 km (7.95 miles)
Map: Landranger 88 Tyneside & Durham area.
                        Pathfinder inaccurate, out of date
Facilities: Full eating and service facilities in Durham, shop
                        (ice cream & chocolate) at Finchale Priory

PLOTTING PLAN	App.	Map ref.	Dep.
START: Framwellgate carpark, A691	-	271428	S
Sewerage works junction	WSW	277432	NE
The Scrogs (wood)	SSW	283445	NNE
H M Prison, Frankland	S	288458	E
Finchale Priory (cross R Wear)	W	296471	N
Cocken road end (TJTL)	E	275472	S
Newton Grange (pub)	NNW	277457	E
H M Prison, Frankland	W	288458	S
Diamond Terrace, bear right	ENE	274430	WSW
FINISH: Framwellgate, A691, care	ENE	271428	-

One wonders if the siting of one of the north's largest prisons and the biggest remand centre so close to one of the oldest priories is accidental or part of a grander plan. Either way Finchale Priory, which I always called Abbey, is worth a visit and the bridleways from Durham City to Frankland worth travelling.

This is a good starter route for adults, the majority of the route being on tarmac in the shape of quiet country roads, but there is sufficient loose surface to demand a mountain bike. We use the rough stuff twice, so the toil of the outward leg is rewarded in full by actually zooming down the same tracks on the way home.

THE RIDE – DURHAM to FINCHALE

There is a huge concrete carpark right on the riverside at Durham, but we used the open-air version on Framwellgate beneath the railway station – it is a lot cheaper! Depart south down the hill from the rough carpark, straight on at the roundabout following the signpost for the riverside, under the concrete carpark then left along the riverbank. All the major services seem to have gravitated to this location, gas, electric, the dole, (sorry DSS), and the water company in the shape of the sewerage treatment works, where we dodge left and right along the perimeter fence and burst out into open farmland within a mile of the start.

Frankland Farm is the immediate destination, but the bridleway quits the tarmac at the far end of the first field and hugs the riverbank, only to rejoin the same road 390 m farther on. A blue bridleway arrow on a wooden gatepost gives you a clue, but the track is only 30 cm wide. The fishermen of the Dunelm Angling Club use the same track to gain access to their water so it is usually smooth and well trodden, although the push around the edge of the field back to the farm access road might be a bit of a trial in the early part of the year. Everyone seems to miss the turn and ride straight along the tarmac! The hill up to the farm may develop the first sweat of the day. The bridleway becomes ash in the farmyard, then stony single track as you climb past The Scrogs wood.

The track weaves through the woods then becomes twin where farm vehicles need access to the fields, and eventually rough road beyond the old railway which persists all the way to Frankland Prison. (Take care in wet weather, some of the potholes are quite deep with sharp edges.) When you reach the tarmac, turn right then left for

Finchale Priory at a strange little roundabout which seems to be nothing more than a turning facility for visitors to the prison.

On the way to Finchale you pass an old munitions depot, where nothing remains apart from a large number of domed concrete buildings, provoking lots of silly speculation about possible use like, crees[3] for giant tortoises, homes for mountain bike hermits or a trials course for bikes with 260 inch diameter wheels!

FINCHALE to DURHAM

Finchale Abbey, now given Priory status by English Heritage, was founded in 1110 AD by St. Godric, who first built himself a simple hut about a mile upstream from the present ruins then converted it to a rough wooden chapel. His reputation for sanctity brought so many pilgrims that his wooden chapel was replaced by the first stone building on the site of the present priory, where he lived to the age of 105 and was buried in his own chapel. Construction of the Priory was begun about 1237 with the building of a church and three altars which were consecrated in 1239.

There are many local tales concerning St. Godric and the Devil, but one of the best relates to the theft of the saint's clothes. One cold winter night, when St. Godric was standing praying in the River Wear up to his neck, the Devil was so provoked to see him that he stole away his clothes, which he had left lying on the bank side. Godric detected the petty larceny, and being well aware who the thief was, set about saying aves and paternosters with might and main. This forced the Devil to return the clothes, much against his will, "for though" as Hegg the historian says, "his apparel was so coarse that the Devil would scarce have worn them," it pained him exceedingly to have to be just, even once!

The OS Pathfinder map still shows the bridge from Finchale across the Wear to Cocken Wood as a toll, but this has not been the case since the 1960s. However, the bridge is still a beautiful piece of work and certainly, as far as we are concerned, fulfils a very useful purpose. What awaits at the far side, the 137 steps up and over the

[3] Cree – pigeon dovecot

Finchale Priory, the river Wear and the footbridge
from Cocken Wood.

cliff to the public road, is perhaps not so attractive. When you reach the road, turn left and enjoy the run along to Cocken Bridge.

Turning south at the top of the hill beyond the bridge takes you under the East Coast main line where the bridge abutments and the hedges nearby abound in pinky-purple Himalayan Balsam which may distract you from the sustained climb. The original intention was to use the bridleway that turns west opposite Finchale Abbey Training Centre but at most times of the year it is unridable and the new industrial estate has gobbled up the southern half beyond Hag House farm, so stick with the road and turn left at the Newton Grange following the signs for Finchale Priory back to the lane at Frankland Prison then retrace the rough stuff all the way back to the riverside at Durham.

Ancient Durham C.C. fingerpost at Bolam Village, Route 9.

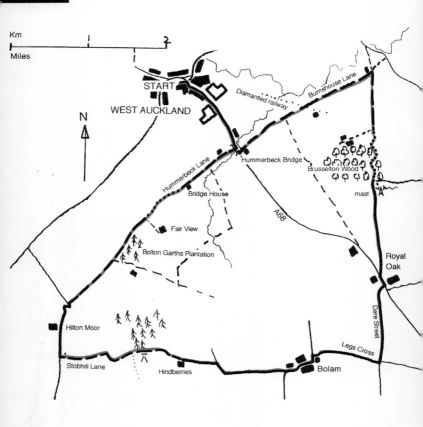

Km

Miles

START

WEST AUCKLAND

N

Dismantled railway

Burnshouse Lane

Hummerbeck Lane

Hummerbeck Bridge

Bridge House

Brusselton Wood

mast

A68

Fair View

Bolton Garths Plantation

Royal Oak

Hilton Moor

Dere Street

Legs Cross

Stobhill Lane

Hindberries

Bolam

9. WEST AUCKLAND

Grade: 3
Total distance: 17.7 km (11.0 miles)
High point: Transmission mast on Dere Street, 216 m
Maps: OS Landranger 92 Barnard Castle & surr. area
OS Landranger 93 Middlesbrough & Darlington
Facilities: Several royally-named pubs, a café and the Crusty Loaf, famous for its pies and sandwiches, all in West Auckland, and The Countryman pub in Bolam village

PLOTTING PLAN	App.	Map ref.	Dep.
START: West Auckland (Parking round edge of green) on A68	-	92/181263	SE
Hummerbeck Bridge	NNW	188254	SW
Bolton Garths Plantation	NE	173240	SW
Stobhill Lane, near Hilton Moor farm	W	168225	E
Bolam, follow unclassified road through village	WSW	198225	ENE
Dere Street, Legs Cross	WNW	93/207226	N
Royal Oak - care crossing A68	S	207239	N
Dere Street, Brusselton Wood	S	205253	N
Burnshouse Lane	NE	203263	SW
Hummerbeck Bridge - care A68	NE	92/188254	NNW
FINISH: West Auckland			

Grading this ride was difficult. The classic dilemma: it isn't very long, has a relatively high percentage of tarmac, but the descent through Brusselton Wood can be fraught with danger, or at the least very exciting for novices, There are low overhanging branches, which have been daubed with high visibility paint to draw attention, and tree roots galore, lethal when wet or covered with leaves like the late October day when I rode it. I thought it was brilliant, but I'm mad.

This is one of those educational routes which I thoroughly enjoy, and there is a fair bit of rough riding too, so if you are out purely for the ride you'll not be disappointed either. Depart south out of West Auckland on the A68 and ride as far as Hummerbeck Bridge, 1.2 km (0.77 miles). However the Cyclists' Touring Club (CTC) British Road Book of 1897 describes it as Humber Bridge, over the Humber Beck and warns that the "surface becomes very bad, and is often under water after heavy rain". Things have improved considerably.

Turn right over a little concrete bridge, past the "Bridleway" signpost and head south-west along Hummerbeck Lane for 3.2 km (2.0 miles). The surface is good as far as Bridge House farm, but immediately beyond the house the road shrinks to single track which can be muddy with a slippery "top" on it throughout the winter months. It is occasionally used by horses, which doesn't do the surface any favours, and I lost traction on one little climb, probably due to the 1.5 inch Specialised Hardpack tyres left on after a race in the Highlands two days before. Bigger knobblies would have eliminated the problem. Roughish tarmac appears at Fair View road end, then there is a steady pull up past Bolton Garths Plantation on a good muddy surface to proper tarmac near Hilton Moor farm.

Turn left with the narrow tarmac past Hilton Moor and keep your eye out for the turn into Stobhill Lane, which will take you east to Bolam village. The distance between Hummerbeck Lane road end and the turn is 0.79 km (0.49 mile). There is no signpost as such, but an alluring "Unsuitable for motors" hidden in the hedge, which you probably wouldn't see approaching from the north.

Just over a kilometre into Stobhill Lane our road goes straight ahead through a pair of ancient stone gateposts onto rougher twin track, but notice the post on the right, it bears a benchmark. A benchmark is a map maker's aid, always cut into rock or stone, often on churches or bridges, things which are unlikely to be pulled down. A gatepost is much rarer. The benchmark consists of a wedge-like horizontal notch surmounting a broad arrow, the sign of the War Department, which originally controlled the Ordnance Survey, and indicates an ascertained height or level. When a surveyor is 'levelling' he fits an angle iron into the notch as a 'bench' or support for his levelling staff and works from this known benchmark.

Watch out for the dogs at Hindberries farm, the young collie looks as if it fancies a bite! Take your time through Bolam, which is one of the prettiest villages in County Durham, then head east to Legs Cross (I was frightened to research the origins of the name!) crossroads on the old Roman road of Dere Street, where you turn north to Royal Oak. This being an old Roman road and trade route for many years, I thought Royal Oak must have some interesting heritage, but, according to the "History of Durham" by MacKenzie and Ross, published in 1834 "Royal Oak is a hamlet deriving its name from the sign of a public house." The pub no longer exists but is mentioned in the CTC Road Book of 1897.

Care crossing the A68, then continue due north on Dere Street, known locally as "The Street", signpost "Shildon", past the transmission mast to the brow of the hill and pause to admire the panoramic view of Bishop Auckland and West Auckland away to the left. This is the technical bit, Brusselton Wood. The track weaves its way down through the trees for 750 metres. Crash helmet and glasses are essential, and watch out for the roots, whinnies and overhanging branches. Great fun. Go straight on with the farm road when you exit the trees, then turn left onto more single track back to Hummerbeck Bridge when the farm road sweeps right towards the main road. The only slight temptation to deviate might arise when you cross an old railway – head straight on.

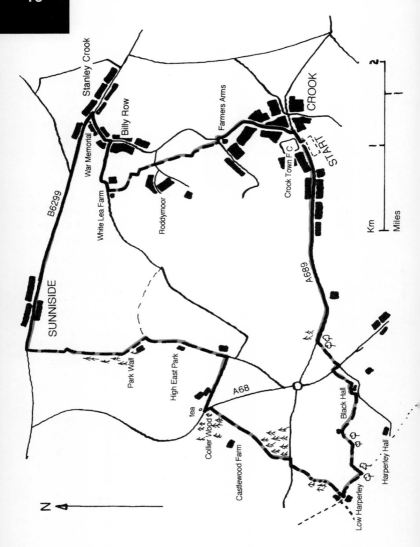

52

10. CROOK & SUNNISIDE

Grade: 3

Total distance: 16.8 km (10.5 miles) Off-road constituent 8.3 km (5.2 miles)

High point: B6299, Sunniside 302 m

Maps: OS Pathfinder 580 Crook & West Auckland
OS Landranger 92 Barnard Castle

Facilities: Full facilities in Crook, pub grub at the Royal George, Billy Row, the Comedian and the Top House (Crown Hotel), Sunniside and all-year tea stop at Jean's caravan on the A68, opposite Collier Wood.

PLOTTING PLAN	App	Map ref	Dep
START: Millfield, Crook, opp. football ground	-	162354	NE
Farmers Arms	SE	161363	NNW
White Lea Farm	S	156375	E
War Memorial, B6299, Stanley Crook	SW	164378	NW
Sunniside	E	136385	S
A68, Collier Wood	SW	130365	SW
Low Harperley	NE	120349	SE
Black Hall	W	131348	NE
A689	SW	137352	ESE
FINISH: Millfield, Crook	WSW	162354	-

Parking directly opposite Millfield, the home of Crook Town Football Club, for many years one of the finest amateur teams in the country, reminds you of the heritage of this part of the world; but today biking is the interest, and route finding the name of the game. There are more gates than normal, so it could be a good idea to do the route with a mate or two to maintain the flow, but on the other hand navigating your own way around and through the fields will bring its own rewards.

You are on the western edge of the Durham coalfield out here, but also the fringe of some magnificent scenery with views up the Weardale to the Pennines, and the ride provides the elevation to appreciate them!

The area is networked, as you might expect in an old mining district, by loads of bridleways, footpaths and old roads, some well used and well defined but others less so. You will experience all types as you ride.

CROOK to SUNNISIDE

The hard part comes first. When you are standing in the carpark opposite the football ground you can see a lot of the route, or at least the terrain to be covered, especially the high ridge from Stanley Crook to Sunniside. The height gain is obvious. Once you set off the going is easy as far as the Farmers Arms, after which you turn left and immediately right. Then even the old roads and bridleways past Roddymoor are easy, at least initially. You wonder when the climb will bite, but bite it does.

The first little kick comes soon after you cross the road to Roddymoor (keep straight on: avoid a left turn), then there's a respite as you weave across the long defunct railway line, followed by another little climb to White Lea Farm. Here turn right to Billy Row. You've nibbled but the killer comes when you turn left into West Terrace at Billy Row. The seats by the war memorial at Stanley Crook may well have been provided for knackered cyclists!

There was a moderate westerly wind as I crept up to Sunniside to be greeted by a pub called The Comedian – obviously someone has a wicked sense of humour; you must be fond of a laugh coming all the way up here for a pint.

SUNNISIDE and HARPERLEY

The real enjoyment starts just west of the village, or it may simply be relief because it is downhill. Turn left over a cattle grid past a sign warning you that "Motorsport is Dangerous" and follow the farm road down past the motocross course with ever increasing speed, taking care at Park Wall farm where you go straight on past the front of the house then through a gate to a junction with a concrete road once used by the opencast coalmine. Turn right and follow the obvious line to High East Park with its all-weather training track for the horses and eventually along to the scrapyard where you turn right along to the A68 and the refreshment caravan opposite Collier Wood.

Care when crossing the A68, then it's a great hurtle down past Castlewood Farm and around to the A689. I can recall shooting down here in a rally car many years ago, but I think it is faster on a bike! When you reach the main road turn right then left in 50 m onto a bridleway through a cornfield. The farmer has left the required width so please stick to it and don't ride on the crops. At the far side of the field the bridleway goes down the left side of the wood – don't be lured over the stile onto the footpath that runs parallel. There is no track alongside the first field, so stick close to the fence, but then you join a rutted field road down to Low Harperley, a rather splendid old farmhouse.

When the railway was built up the Wear Valley at the end of the last century, there was virtually nothing here but a park and a mansion, something which hasn't changed much. Part of the hard bargaining that allowed the railway to be built along the fringe of the park was the building of a station for the convenience of the landowner. It can't have seen much use and is long gone, but the railway remains, still hauling cement from higher up the valley.

As soon as you enter the farmyard at Low Harperley turn left out again, through a gate that leads into the pleasant parkland, then left

War memorial and view down over Crook and the Wear Valley.

again at the first opportunity just over 300 m later through a gate marked with a yellow arrow. The bridleway now weaves its way along the edge of the fields to Black Hall, where it is tempting to use the tarmac access road for the Durham Police establishment at Harperley Hall, but the bridleway weaves its way around the back of the houses and up to the A68 again on a good loose road.

Turn right then first left for the sting in the tail, the short loose climb up to the A689. Laneside vegetation encroaches onto the track at the height of summer making constant lane change essential if you are to avoid extensive scratching, but once you turn right onto the main road and crest the last hill it is downhill all the way to the finish. The only dangers are chilling and exceeding the speed limit as you enter Crook.

The parkland bridleway near Low Harperley.

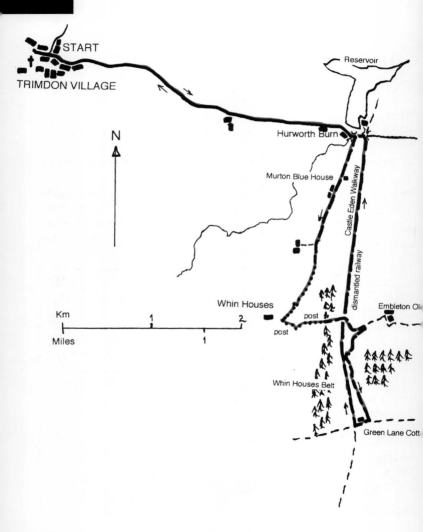

START

TRIMDON VILLAGE

Reservoir

Hurworth Burn

Murton Blue House

Castle Eden Walkway

dismantled railway

N

Whin Houses

post

post

Embleton Ol

Km   1   2

Miles   1

Whin Houses Belt

Green Lane Cott

11. TRIMDON WHINS

Grade:	3
Total distance:	16.75 km (10.41 miles)
High Point:	Trimdon Village, 145 m
Map:	OS Landranger 93 Middlesbrough & Darlington area
Facilities:	All in Trimdon, Red Lion, Fox & Hounds, Black Bull
Note:	This is a summer route only, for no other reason than that the mud hereabouts is incredibly glutinous, so much so it jammed the front wheel completely on a December tour. If it is wet, or has been wet, forget it.

PLOTTING PLAN	App.	Map Ref.	Dep.
START: Opposite Red Lion, Front Street, Trimdon Village	-	93/372342	ESE
Hurworth Burn bridge	NW	408332	SSW
Field boundary	N	403316	WSW
Wood	W	405311	E
Embleton Old Hall farm road	NW	408310	SW
Castle Eden Walkway, Green Lane Cottages	ENE	408299	N
Dismantled railway, Castle Eden Walkway	S	407315	N
Hurworth Burn railway bridge, quit Walkway	S	409332	W
FINISH: Front Street, Trimdon Village	ESE	372342	-

Say Trimdon to anyone brought up in the Durham & Northumberland coalfield and the mining explosion of 1882, when a total of 83 men and boys died, comes immediately to mind. A stranger, nowadays, would find very little to give him a clue to the great mining tradition of the Trimdons, Trimdon Village, Trimdon Grange, (scene of the disaster), or Trimdon Station, but the history of the place goes back a lot further than the industrial era.

The Boldon Book, or as it was originally 'Buke', a kind of County Durham Domesday Book, which was compiled in 1180, records the village as Tremeduna, the name currently accorded to the sheltered accommodation near the Norman church, where incidentally we parked the car. One theory is that the name derived from the time when King Canute, or Cnut, got off his horse at this spot, had his head shaved and made a barefoot pilgrimage to the shrine of St. Cuthbert at Durham. The reason for the penitent walk has been lost in time, although historians will tell you there was a wide choice of sins for him to repent!

The 'whin' aspect of the ride title alludes both to the derelict Whin Houses which mark the point where you turn east towards the old railway, and also to the gorse you will surely encounter *en route*. Whin or whinnies is a fairly common name for gorse in our part of the world, particularly in rural areas.

THE RIDE

This is a ride of two halves: a bridleway section through fields surrounding the old Castle Eden Branch line, and then the return along the old railway itself which now comprises part of the Castle Eden Walkway.

Trimdon was chosen for refreshment, interest and because there is no convenient parking at the northern end of the Walkway near Hurworth Burn. The run down to the bridleway at Hurworth Burn is a good warm up, but alas the toil back up the hill at the end of the ride might be less welcome. Grit your teeth, it's all good training!

The Red Lion was purely a nominal starting point to give you a distance to the turn-off for Murton Blue House, 4. 04 km (2.51 miles), the first bridleway. You shouldn't miss it, as it is immediately east of the single lane Hurworth Burn Bridge, although the signpost saying "Footpath", when the track is actually a bridleway, might give you cause for concern.

There are signs asking you to slow down for horses at Murton Blue House, then a galvanised gate past a fine duck pond leads into a lane and then across a huge field after a second gate. This was the glutinous bit, it should be ridable in summer. When you reach the far side of the field turn right to the gate, with a fine modern fastening designed to ease passage for horse riders, then left through it and down the hedge to the next one.

A little navigational ability is now required. The bridleway continues in a straight line across the field, but ours turns very sharp left, about opposite Whin Houses, before reaching the next fence, and drops down to a burn which is surrounded by whins. There are substantial posts bearing blue bridleway arrows to guide you east, but until you see the first one in the middle of the field a tight left turn for no apparent reason might seem a little strange. The burn, like the whins, is a bit problematic!

The posts will lead you to and through the narrow wood, Whin Houses Belt, then gates and bridleway arrows take you onwards through a cutting in the railway and around the edge of what was a turnip field to the Embleton Old Hall farm road where you turn sharp right. At the third corner the bridleway leaves the farm road keeping close to the railway embankment, then rejoins it 200 m farther on. Eventually you reach a farm track T-junction, where you turn right past a white house, Green Lane Cottages, then right again up onto the railway path.

This last section was supposed to be an easy run home, and probably is at the height of summer, but two days after the snow had melted it was hard work. The surface was soft, allowing the tyres to sink in about a centimetre, and what would normally be the hard bits – the little climbs where bridges have been removed – turned out to be no more difficult than the rest. We arrived at Hurworth Burn in a full sweat, which didn't diminish at all on the final pull up to Trimdon Village.

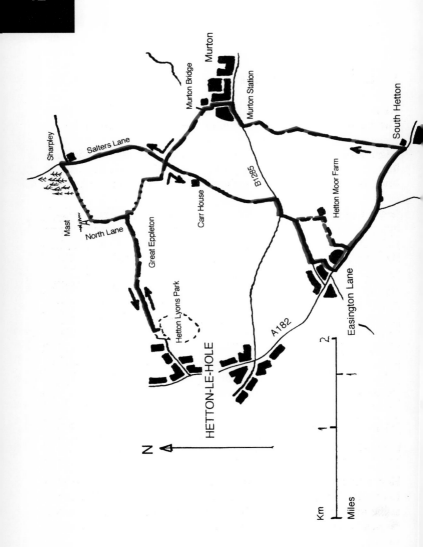

12. HETTON & MURTON

Grade: 3
Total distance: 13.0 km (8.1 miles). Off-road constituent 7.3 km (4.5 miles)
High point: North Lane, near Great Eppleton Farm, 150 m
Maps: OS Landranger 88 Tyneside & Durham area
Facilities: Fish & chip shops in Hetton le Hole and Murton

PLOTTING PLAN	App.	Map ref.	Dep.
START: Hetton Lyons park	-	359480	E
Great Eppleton farm	WSW	371482	SE
Salter's Lane, N of Carr House farm	W	377478	WSW
B1285	N	372466	SW
South Hetton	NW	378452	N
Murton Station, B1285	S	381470	NE
Murton Bridge	SE	383475	NW
Salter's Lane, N of Carr House farm	ESE	377478	NE
Sharpley Plantations	S	376489	SW
FINISH: Hetton Lyons park	ENE	359480	-

Hetton Lyons park has been created upon the site of the former Hetton Lyons and Eppleton collieries. This ride is more a tour of industrial archeology than a mountain bike challenge. The district was a vast mining complex for well over a hundred years, the truly enormous pit heaps the most lasting testament to the labour of the men. Despite landscaping and great efforts to re-vegetate the surrounds, the legacy remains. It's not something we should forget.

When you tour the area on a bike you see at close quarters the remains, not only of the pits and coke works, but the railways that carried the coal and inevitably the tracks and footpaths that the miners used to get to work and latterly walk for recreation. It will be very unusual if you don't meet a couple of marras[4] continuing to enjoy the fresh air. This isn't the prettiest ride in the book, but is one I urge you to take.

HETTON LE HOLE to EASINGTON LANE

Jeff Rutter and I did this one cold winter day – one of those days when you really don't want to turn out, but having done so, come home with a satisfied glow. The warden of the sports facilities at Hetton Lyons park was sheltering in his office, huddled over a tiny fire, and I think he thought we were fond of a treat setting off in such threatening weather.

There is ample space for cars at the park, which is often the venue for cycle races of all descriptions, both on and off road throughout the year.

Make your way back up to the tarmac road and turn right towards Great Eppleton farm. It is a bit of a cruel start, climbing up to just about the highest point on the route at the very beginning, but it warmed us quite nicely by the time we hit the rough stuff. There is a sign at the top of the hill informing the public that this is a private road, but it carries bridleway status, so is fine for bikes. The farmyard was slimy and clarty[5]; then when we reached the stile at the bottom of North Lane, which runs down from the transmission mast, the entrance to the field was ankle deep mud! This should be a lot better in summer, but it was a pair of delicate pedestrians who turned right and followed the track next to the hedge around the field. The track is little used, even by the tractors, and is a bit bumpy. However, it only lasts for 480 m until a "Bridleway" sign points you right, through a gate into a loose hedge-fringed lane. There is a pond on the left

[4] Marras – mates, close friends
[5] Clarty – muddy, dirty

which obviously attracts a fair amount of wildlife, and we saw a firecrest, the smallest European bird, at the burn in the dip.

The track turns left up to Salter's Lane, which again will probably be fine in summer, but melting snow had it running with freezing water. Things improve greatly when you reach the minor crossroads north of Carr House farm, then as you turn right to ride south to the B1285 the surface improves again to typical farm road. Beyond Carr House you cross a dismantled railway which served the Hetton collieries.

Perhaps strangely this district is also known for its fairies. In the last century "everybody knew it, hundreds had heard them," piping, fiddling, singing and dancing far underground. There was a famous circular mound between Eppleton and Hetton, consisting entirely of field stones, with a little hollow in the top called the Fairies' Cradle. Here the fairies used to dance, to music made on a peculiarly sweet-toned pipe by a supernatural minstrel. If it is dead still and quiet, why not stop, put your ear to the ground and listen.

When we reached the B1285 we turned right, then left towards Easington Lane, then straight on at the first corner onto a rough road to the old Hetton Moor Farm, which is now a scrapyard, and eventually out into the eastern fringe of Easington Lane, but it isn't really worth it due to the risk of puncture from all the rubbish lying around. The sensible , but ´tarmac´, thing to do is simply follow the back road WSW to the A182 and then ride south-east through Easington Lane to South Hetton.

SOUTH HETTON to HETTON LYONS
Turn left at the Station Hotel, South Hetton´, and follow the line of the railway which can be seen stretching away into the distance. Initially the road is concrete, but this soon becomes packed earth as it climbs past the allotments. It then becomes twin track up the side of fields, bears right then left through a hole in the hedge, across a path left through the crops by the farmer and then more or less north with the power lines to Murton. Someone keeps horses in one paddock so take care to close the garden gates after you pass!

Food and shelter, an ideal lunch stop.

Turn right onto the main road (B1285) through Murton, left after 330 m to pass the chip shop and post office, left over the speed humps into Dowson Square and eventually over the old railway bridge, Murton Bridge, past the football pitch. Then continue straight ahead along the obvious bridleway to an interesting section through the wood and eventually back to Salter's Lane.

You will recognise the rough crossroads at Salter's Lane having approached from the opposite direction earlier, but this time turn north and ride all the way to Sharpley Plantations. The final leg lies south-west to and through Great Eppleton, down the south side of the wood, up the fieldside track to the mast, then south down North Lane to the farm and over the hill to Hetton Lyons park.

We were so dirty when we finished that the warden broke out his hosepipe for us. A gentleman.

Sculpture from old railway materials near Chester-le-Street, Route 13.

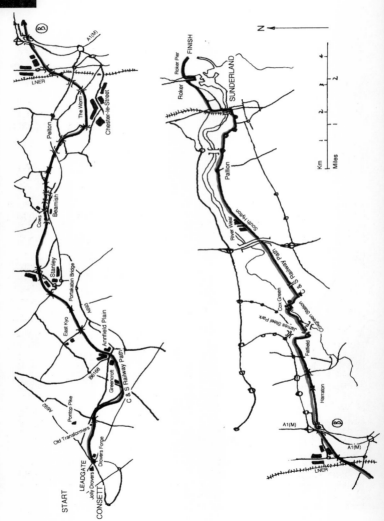

13. CONSETT & SUNDERLAND RAILWAY PATH

Grade: 3
Total distance: 36.3 km (22.6 miles)
High point: Railway path 300 metres before Greencroft crossroads, 260 m. Start, Jolly Drovers, Leadgate, 253 m
Maps: OS Landranger 88 Tyneside & Durham
Facilities: Pub grub at the Jolly Drovers, Leadgate. Bungalow Café and Raffaele's Pizzeria, Roker, near finish.

PLOTTING PLAN	App.	Map ref.	Dep.
START: Jolly Drovers roundabout, Leadgate	-	88/133519	ENE
Annfield Plain, B6168	SW	171513	NNE
Stanley. A6076 overbridge	WSW	200538	ENE
Pelton, still C & S Railway Path	NNW	250526	SSE
LNER Main East Coast Line overbridge	SSW	271532	NNE
Harraton, C & S Railway Path	WSW	296544	ENE
Fatfield carpark	NNW	317547	ENE
Cox Green Station, rejoin railway path	NW	330549	NE
Pallion, join tarmac roads. Alternative Finish	WSW	368576	E
Wearmouth Bridge approach	WSW	396572	N
FINISH: Lower promenade, Roker	NNW	409585	-

Having just put in the hardest ride in months, according this route an objective grade became quite difficult. The route is downhill virtually all the way from Leadgate to the coast and most of the railway path has an excellent surface, totally non-technical and, until you reach Pallion totally traffic free, so the only factor raising it from Grade 1 must be the distance. At least that would be the case in normal conditions, however, the day of the ride it was so cold – something in the order of minus 5 Centigrade at Leadgate and little better at the coast; and there had been a reasonable snowfall in the days preceding, producing heavily iced tracks for most of the way that were barely ridable for the first eleven kilometres – that a grading on the day must have been at least 9, perhaps even as high as 12! Bear this in mind for any route.

We parked at the Jolly Drovers, Leadgate, but as soon as I stepped out of the car I slipped and was only saved the most ignominious start by grabbing the roof rack. Pam was going to drive to Roker and wait for me there, and was pleased to leave the icy wastes of Consett, especially after a lady in a 4 X 4 nearly wrote her off in the carpark while she was giving me a few minutes to turn back.

Turn back! I must confess it crossed my mind in the first 100 metres! This section of the Consett & Sunderland Railway Path starts at the roundabout on the A692 by weaving its way through "The Maze" an intriguing feature carved from the old pithead of Leadgate's Eden Colliery. In summer this tight test of riding skill is great entertainment, but bedded with frozen ice akin to lumpy glass it was murder. The sides of the maze are so steep you can't ride up them and the ice was so slippery that even the Continental Premolars, currently the best snow and mud tyre available, were totally ineffective, although they did prove their worth over the rest of the route.

My theory was that it would become easier as the altitude diminished and I neared the coast. What a load of rubbish, I was riding through snow and ice all the way to Pallion. Well, OK it did get easier, because I managed to actually get on the bike and ride after 200 metres, lowest gears on the granny ring, but at least I was riding. I was just about coming to terms with the amount of effort required when I met a gentleman from Greencroft crunching along with his dog, who raised my spirits a little higher. "By you're a hard man, there's been nobody along here with a bike for three days. How far are you going?" The board at the Drovers Forge had said 22 miles (36 km) and it was right. The only decent thing about that first 3.5 km had been a spectacular flock of yellow hammers, something I'd never seen before, and the crack with the Squire of Greencroft. Even the Old Transformers looked frozen.

When you meet the A693 at Greencroft crossroads there is a particularly confusing signpost for the cycle route. The old railway lies diagonally opposite, just look for the obvious route of the railway, cross both the unclassified road then the A693 and ride away from the Annfield Plain bypass. The railway cuts straight through the middle of the town. There are distractions galore *en route* to the coast, even here, as you pass the last heather, there are BMX hills to test your power explosion ability if you so desire, but on that late November day they had frozen ponds surrounding them and I was expending far too much energy as it was.

The most reliable signpost in Annfield Plain is the little C2C plaque directly opposite the Co-op supermarket. Cross the road via the complicated central refuge and head nor-nor-east with the railway, on 17.5 km (10.9 miles) of unbroken railway path. Not even a road crossing. Once past the pigeon crees[7] on the edge of town there is a long gentle downhill, over the open bridge near East Kyo where you would turn off if you were doing the Pontop route, then on through the thundering Portakabin bridge north-west of Stanley. From a distance your heart might sink when you see the apparently inevitable rise into Stanley, but in the best railway tradition the old railway maintains a gentle gradient, skirting the town on the north side.

The line to Consett steelworks was always regarded as twisty and steep, this section especially so. It wasn't unusual in the days of steam for trains to stop at Beamish for a "blow up" – in other words build up a full head of steam – before tackling this final sustained slog, even if both fireman and driver had been shovelling coal as

[7] Cree – dovecot

71

hard as they could. As you ride through the now heavily wooded cutting at Beamish, try to picture the scene. The biggest bridge is still smoke blackened, as result of trains making a supreme effort.

Next landmarks are the incredible metal cows in the long cutting at Beamish; then for me an entertaining and stunning flock of goldfinches as I approached Pelton, leading to the major earthwork sculpture of "The Worm" in the old marshalling yard at Chester-le-Street. Even in the snow, someone had ridden the ridge of the Worm's back, a tremendous bit of skill. I was content with breaking the ice on the pools at it's foot. (You see, it was getting warmer, this was the first ice I had actually fractured!)

In spring you will see a fine selection of blossom near where the old signal box used to stand – from cherry, apple, lilac and the remnants of herbaceous plants that surrounded the trackside buildings.

Another resounding footbridge crosses the main east coast line at Birtley, followed immediately by the impressive refraction columns of the British Oxygen Company's site. Then, as you ride under the bridge beyond the A1(M), you are confronted with a choice, higher or lower. I took the lower which is obviously the old railway, but found myself riding across iced-up pools and dodging debris. In fairly deep snow it was impossible to tell, but the higher route has been surfaced and unless you are a purist, the obvious route to take. I had forgotten about this.

When Adrian Gidney and I first designed the off-road Coast to Coast from Whitehaven to Roker Pier in 1992, the old railway east of the school at Fatfield wasn't a path. It was a case of riding through rubbish and rubble, sneaking alongside the current railway, climbing the embankment then fiddling your way down into the James Steel Park to cross the River Wear at Cox Green. Now it is a lot easier, the rubbly track is a pukka path which bears right at the allotments, then weaves its way south down the edge of the housing estate to the Fatfield carpark where you turn left under the railway bridge, through the Park and along to the Cox Green bridge. Most of it is signed C2C. If in doubt aim for the river and head downstream.

After you cross the river, turn left then right uphill at the Oddfellows Arms, signpost Coxgreen Station. By this time my feet were frozen, so as soon as the hill started to bite I got off and walked, in an effort to exercise some life back into my toes. I even walked the flat bit up to the last old railway at the station house. Feet rejuvenated, I turned left onto what used to be signposted "River Wear Trail" but now has "C2C Sunderland", for the last off-road to Pallion. Despite sights like the Nissan site across the river to the north, and eventually the crane factory which was Coles down below, this final stretch is still very open, even sporting a couple of free range horses on the line near The Hycroft at South Hylton. There's a final flee through the limestone cutting high above the Wear and the run out to the edge of the trading estate at Pallion. This would be a good place to end the ride if you have young riders in the party, and are being met by a chauffeur(euse). It avoids the busy city centre approach roads.

However, to complete the route, join the tarmac at the Rolls Royce factory and continue to head downstream on the south side of the river through five roundabouts, initially following the signs for "City Centre" then "Wearmouth Bridge and South Shields". There is the temptation of the C2C route into the city centre, but as it doesn't go where we want, ignore it. Eventually you weave your way around to the splendid Wearmouth bridges, the impressive railway bridge lying immediately upstream of the road bridge. You will get your first glimpse of the Roker pier as you ride onto the bridge, store the image because that's where you are heading. There is an elaborate one-way system at the north side of the bridge through Monkwearmouth and east out to Roker. Inevitably I turned right into Dundas Street, before the main junction and ended up riding through someone's garden at the end of a cul-de-sac, but you should do it right!

When you reach the seafront at Roker, map reference 88/407587, turn right at a roundabout not marked on the Landranger and down to the lower promenade, left at the bottom and along to the pier. The ride is completed by riding to the lighthouse. Unfortunately the gates were closed in November despite the fact the sea was like a mill pond. The weather guessers must have got it wrong, again.

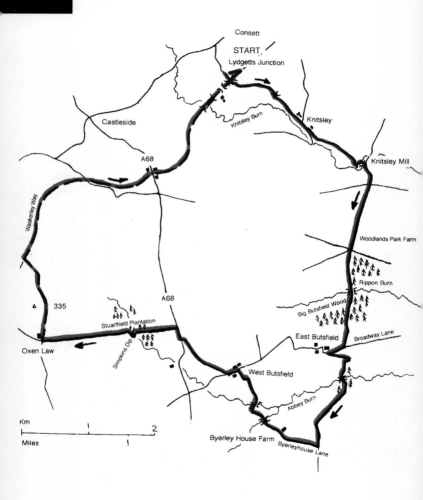

Consett

START
Lydgetts Junction

Castleside

A68

Knitsley Burn

Knitsley

Knitsley Mill

Waskerley Way

Woodlands Park Farm

Rippon Burn

335

Big Butsfield Wood

Stuartfield Plantation

A68

East Butsfield

Broadway Lane

Oxen Law

Simpkins Dip

West Butsfield

Abbey Burn

Km

1

2

Miles

1

Byerley House Farm

Byerleyhouse Lane

14. KNITSLEY & BUTSFIELD

Grade: 4
Total distance: 19.7 km (12.2 miles)
High point: Green road north of Oxen Law, 335 m
Maps: OS Landranger 88 Tyneside & Durham area
OS Landranger 87 Hexham, Haltwhistle & surrounding area, but not really necessary, 99.5% of the ride on sheet 88. The sketch map will suffice.
Facilities: Large carpark at Lydgetts junction, signposted as a picnic area from the A692 between Consett and Castleside. No refreshments on route. This is remarkably wild and remote countryside.

PLOTTING PLAN	App.	Map ref.	Dep.
START: Lydgetts Junction carpark, near Howns Farm	-	88/098495	SE
Knitsley	WNW	114484	ESE
Woodlands	NNE	119474	SSW
East Butsfield hairpin	NE	115452	ESE
Byerleyhouse Lane	SE	105441	NW
Stuartfield crossroads, A68	SSE	091455	W
Oxen Law, green road	SSE	071466	NNW
Waskerley Way	SE	87/068465	NNE
Waskerley Way, Rowley, A68	SW	88/087479	ENE
FINISH: Waskerley Way, Lydgetts Junction	SW	099494	-

If you don't like hills don't do this one. I actually found the route marked on an old Ordnance Survey map – it was the first few miles of a motor rally, probably organised by either Consett or Whickham & District Motor Club in the seventies. Try to imagine yourself tearing down these lanes in an Escort Twin Cam in the dead of night. Believe me it really focused the mind, was highly exciting and not without danger if you got it wrong. Geordie rallying in those days was matched only by the tarmac road races held in Wales, but faster!

Obviously the off-road section of the route across the moor above Oxen Law and then along the Waskerley Way wasn't in the rally route – some of the railway was still working. In fact I can recall, probably at an earlier date, weaving down these lanes through the giant Consett Iron Works complex with steam and flame colouring the night sky, a living example of Blake's Satanic mills. Turner should have painted the scene. It was brilliant.

The road section of the ride cuts across the western catchment area of the River Browney, which forms the Lanchester Valley. The first watercourse crossed is the Knitsley Burn which joins the Browney proper just east of Lanchester; next is the Rippon Burn which meets the river at Browney Bridge downstream of East Butsfield; then two crossings of the Abbey Burn, the first at the little confluence at Browney Bridge, then again downhill from Byerley House farm at Byerleyhouse Bridge. This is followed by two crossings of the Black Burn, firstly 300 m after Byerleyhouse Bridge then again west of the A68 at Simpkins dip, near Stuartfield Plantation. It might be tarmac but the first half is either down, or up.

THE RIDE

Depart south-east from the Lydgetts Junction carpark under the high but narrow bridge, often through a large puddle, immediately left and right and downhill to jink right and left over another railway. There is slight complication at Knitsley, so go slightly right at the first junction then slightly left at the next, not down the hill, yet!

The road maintains height immediately to the east of Knitsley then descends with increasing speed, culminating in the very tight hairpins above Knitsley Mill. Watch what you are doing, you could run into the side of the house!

Turn right at the T-junction at the trout fishery, gently up to the crossroads, then climb steeply straight on, signpost "Satley". The road up past Woodlands is bordered by substantial stone walls and you start to get that moorland feel.

A signpost "Butsfield" shows the way ahead at the five lane ends, the road shrinks, and there is a great scoot downhill to the Rippon Burn, across what was a muddy, leafy bridge and up through the forestry of Big Butsfield wood. Perhaps the trees weren't as big in the rallying days, but visibility is restricted on the bike, it must have been extremely limited in a fast car.

Turn right at the aptly named Broadway Lane to East Butsfield, which in reality is only a hamlet surrounding a large farm, then hairpin left in 150 metres. You can cut the corner on a loose muddy track, but make sure you can see if anything is coming up the hill – says he who nearly had a confrontation with the postman! Stick with the tarmac on the next hairpin right and shoot down to the Abbey Burn, where the bridge is a bit problematic and can easily rob you of impetus for the forthcoming climb. By this time I was beginning to fade, ascent wise!

The next right turn towards West Butsfield along Byerleyhouse Lane isn't signposted, but it is the first on the right and not difficult to find. This leads into a colourful descent over the Abbey Burn again, with another bridge where I ran wide, or was I just losing the bottle with the leaves? West Butsfield brings a little relief, the road being level after you turn west and almost immediately north-west at a right fork, then a reasonable climb to the A68 at Stuartfield. There's only 100 metres north on the A68 to the crossroads where we turn west, the only signpost being "B & B" at Bee Cottage Farm. The flash down to the final stream crossing, the Black Burn, coincides with Simpkins dip.

Sam Simpkins was a championship winning rally navigator who lived not too far from here and was good enough to warn me of the severity of the bends in the bottom. The Landranger map still shows

Looking to share the sandwiches near Butsfield Abbey.

the deviation as a very slight left, right, left, but the reality is considerably different, especially at 60 mph! Many cars came to grief in the bottom. You'll even need to watch it on the bike, grit and gravel tend to accumulate in the dip.

Oxen Law farm is "ripe for renovation", a term some might level at the road that heads north to the highest point on the route. For us it is great entertainment, gradually changing from a loose stone surface to grass and a splendid ride across the moor to the old railway which comprises the Waskerley Way. Enjoy the railway all the way back to Lydgetts Junction, a stretch culminating in a crossing of the so impressive Howns Farm Viaduct. You'll enjoy this one.

The `Old Transformer´ near East Castle, Route 15.

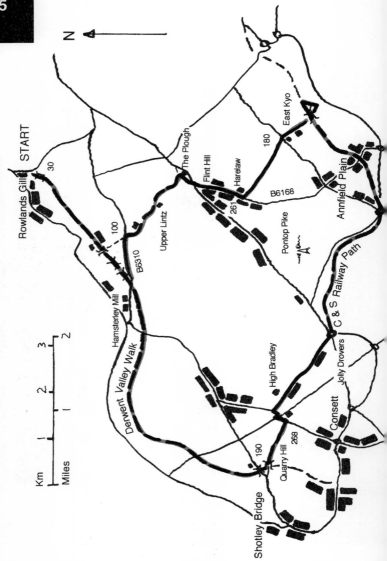

N

START
Rowlands Gills
30
100
B6310
Upper Lintz
The Plough
Flint Hill
Harelaw
261
East Kyo
180
B6168
Pontop Pike
Annfield Plain
Hamsterley Mill
Derwent Valley Walk
High Bradley
C & S Railway Path
Jolly Drovers
Consett
268
Quarry Hill
190
Shotley Bridge

Km
Miles
3   2   1
2   1

15. PONTOP

Grade: 4
Total distance: 28.6 km (17.8 miles)
High points: B6308, Hat & Feather Inn, Medomsley, 268 m.
Railway path betw. Leadgate & Annfield Plain all
around 250 m contour. B6168 at Poplar Grove,
Harelaw, 261 m
Map: OS Landranger 88 Tyneside & Durham area
Facilities: Carpark at Stirling Lane, Rowlands Gill. Several
pubs on the route, most doing pub grub.

PLOTTING PLAN	App.	Map ref.	Dep.
START: Rowlands Gill	-	88/167581	SSW
B6310, Hamsterley Mill	NE	142561	WSW
Derwent Valley Walk	NE	111559	SSW
Summerhill, Shotley Bridge	NNW	104532	ESE
Quarry Hill	WNW	110530	ESE
Pont Lane, High Bradley	NW	118530	SE
Consett & Sunderland Railway Path, Leadgate	WSW	135520	ENE
C & S Railway Path, Annfield Plain	WSW	165511	ENE
East Kyo railway bridge	SW	180524	NW
Poplar Grove, B6168, Harelaw	SE	162538	NNE
Upper Lintz	SSE	164553	NNW
B6310, Hamsterley Mill, rejoin Derwent Walk	ENE	142561	NE
FINISH: Rowlands Gill	SW	167581	-

The magnificent railway paths created by Durham County Council provide off-road arteries through some of the most densely populated parts of the county. It is quite difficult to join them to create a circular tour, but it can be done. Inevitably this involves tarmac and often hopping between centres of population, but in this case the steep downhills and severe climbs linking the off-road railways are all asphalt which eases the pain of the ascents, which is no little bonus when you look at the map. If you need any convincing on the height factor of this ride consider the fact that Pontop Pike, the first television transmitter in this part of the world, sits on the highest point of the route. Choose reasonable weather for the ride – it will make a considerable difference.

THE RIDE

Join the Derwent Walk railway route at the B6314 and head towards Consett. The gentle climb and firm surface provide an excellent warm-up before the real climbing begins. There is an inkling of what lies ahead when you cross the B6310 at Medomsley Bank after 4.5 km (2.8 miles) and see the road snaking up the hill. Prior to this take note when you cross the B6310 at Hamsterley Mill shortly after the twin viaducts, because this is where you rejoin the Derwent Walk on the homeward leg.

Shotley Bridge station, originally called Snows Green, lies 9.8 km (6.1 miles) up the line from Rowlands Gill, is well marked and has two bridges in quick succession. We leave up a steep path at the second to join the tarmac up past the golf course. I thought "they'll love me for this" as I lifted the bike over the awkward stile at the top of the embankment, but it's all part of mountain biking, and you've got a fair bit of tarmac for the next half hour!

I must admit I didn't think it was the highest point on the route, but the T-junction at the top of Quarry Hill turned out to be so. Turn left along to the Hat & Feather, then right and immediately left signposted "Medomsley", opposite the pub, followed by a right within 200 metres towards Bradley Cottages and Leadgate. If in doubt head for the Pontop Pike transmitter! Celtic spear heads were discovered in the fields near High Bradley farm only a hundred years ago. I wonder if they were abandoned there before or after the Romans built the wall some 14 kilometres to the north.

You join the Consett to Sunderland cycle route at the Jolly Drovers roundabout and immediately encounter a maze carved in the old Eden Colliery pit heap. The route from here to Annfield Plain is along a splendid elevated concourse high above the Browney valley, great views and great riding. The nearest point to the Pontop transmitter is marked by the huge industrial sculpture "The Old Transformers", of particular interest to your author, because I used to work on these beasts in the 1950s – part of my apprenticeship at C A Parsons, Newcastle being served in the Transformer shop. I could still detect the distinctive smell of the vegetable-based insulating/cooling oil.

There are a couple of road crossings, at Greencroft and in Annfield Plain itself before you quit the railway at East Kyo railway bridge, map reference 180524. Watch out for it because it has a fast downhill approach, with no sign other than a sole railway sleeper stuck in the ground which probably once bore a notice. If there's no-one about you can actually fly most of the bridge, then anchor up and leave on the right, it's an easier manoeuvre than the weird barriers at the other side.

Having left the railway you now head north-west to Flint Hill, then right on the B6168 through Flint Hill to cross the A692 near The Plough. There's a final bit of rough track between Upper Lintz and the B6310 at Lintz Green where, despite the obvious road straight across which would take you down to Lintz Green Station, we must turn left down towards Hamsterley to rejoin the Derwent Walk before the village. The reason for this absurd manoeuvre is that the road only carries footpath status. Crazy!

Having rejoined the railway it is a mere 3.6 km (2.2 miles) gently downhill to Rowlands Gill.

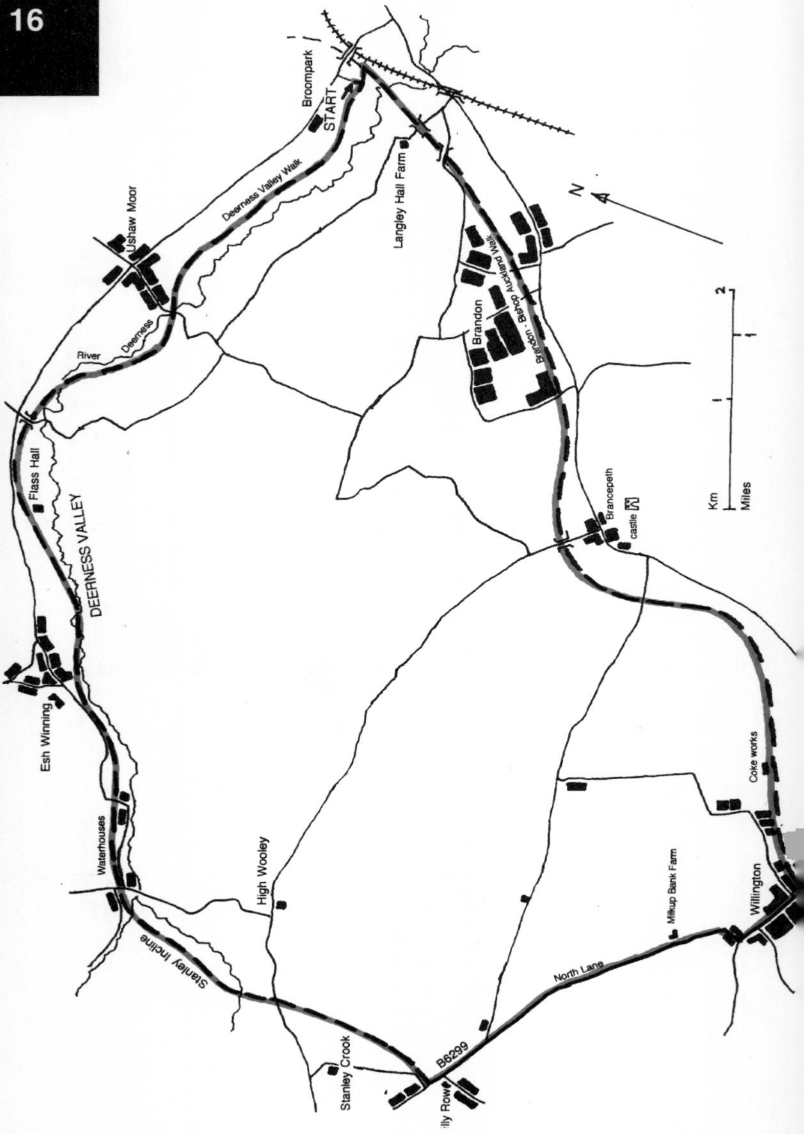

START
Broompark

Deerness Valley Walk

Ushaw Moor

River Deerness

Langley Hall Farm

Brandon

Brandon - Bishop Auckland Walk

N

Flass Hall

DEERNESS VALLEY

Brancepeth
castle

Km
Miles

Esh Winning

Waterhouses

High Wooley

Stanley Incline

Coke works

Millsup Bank Farm

Willington

Stanley Crook

B6299

North Lane

 lly Row

16. DEERNESS VALLEY FULL TOUR

Grade: 4

Total distance: 26.0 km (16.2 miles). Off-road constituent 20.2 km (12.6 miles)

High point: Old school, Stanley Crook, 264 m

Maps: The number of maps looks daunting, but in reality the route is easy to follow, being quite well signposted. You should carry the Landrangers for reassurance, but will need nothing more than the sketchmap. OS Landrangers 88 Tyneside & Durham area, 92 Barnard Castle & surrounding area, 93 Middlesbrough & Darlington area

Facilities: Nothing at Start/Finish but all villages passed *en route* have pubs with grub, & shops selling picnic ingredients. Particularly recommended is the chippy you pass on the main street in Willington.

PLOTTING PLAN	App.	Map ref.	Dep.
START: Broompark picnic area	-	88/251415	W
Esh Winning	ENE	191416	SW
High Wooley	N	92/172389	S
B6299, Billy Row, turn left onto public road	NNE	170374	SE
Willington, rejoin railway path system	NW	199352	NE
Coke Works	SW	93/207358	NE
Brandon	SW	243398	NE
Langley Hall Farm	SW	88/250408	NE
FINISH: Broompark picnic area	E	251425	-

This route combines two of the most southerly railway walks in County Durham, the Deerness Valley Walk, which follows the River Deerness, and part of the Brandon to Bishop Auckland Walk from Willington back through Brandon to Broompark. The going is reasonably easy unless it is blowing a gale!

These paths are not the normal leisurely ride all the way. On the outward leg there is the steep and sustained climb up the Stanley Incline, where a standing engine at the top of the hill used to haul the trucks up, gravity taking them down; and on the return run much of the riding is on fast single track despite the fact that the route lies on the bed of the old railway. The two railway paths are linked by 5.8 km (3.6 miles) of tarmac which includes 2.8 km (1.6 miles) down North Lane from Billy Row to Willington. It is virtually dead straight and very, very fast, close to 80 kph (50 mph) with the following wind on the day we chose, and you'll appreciate the mountain bike brakes at the last corner into Willington.

BROOMPARK to BILLY ROW

The entrance to the picnic area is marked by a brown "Forest Picnic Site" fingerpost, just west of the main railway line, but once you locate the concrete road there is ample room to park. Three railway walks emanate from the wide grassed area at Broompark, the Lanchester Valley Walk which we disregard today, Deerness Valley which is our outward leg, and Brandon to Bishop Auckland which we use as the return route.

Depart W towards Ushaw Moor along the signposted Deerness Valley Walk which clings to the north side of the vale above the river and soon develops an old railway feel. There are the remnants of several small crossings giving access to the steep fields on your left and one is forced to contemplate the dangers of crossing the track with cattle in it's operational days with trains carrying several hundred tons of coal trundling down the valley.

There was a wooden trestle bridge spanning both the Ushaw Moor – Brancepeth road and the river until the 1960s, but now you have a drop and a climb instead. Then you pass beneath a wide road bridge which carries what was once the main road to Flass Hall, the then main settlement in the valley. The road is now very minor but the underside of the bridge is grand. Riveted girders joined by old brick arches look as if they will last for ever, unlike the coal industry which has vanished but left many reminders like the Miners' Hall at Esh Winning, or the church at Waterhouses built of the same off-white bricks so common in the Durham coalfield.

Hamilton Row bridge has been infilled, so you climb up to the road at the back of the pub and then are rewarded with a descent to the start of the Stanley Incline. Sustain the impetus for as long as possible for the track does its best to impede you, throwing in a loose surface to add to the toil, and then near High Wooley it peters out into a narrow grassy climb to a stile. There are no signs to warn you but at 92/172389 you must lift your bike over the stile to cross the tarmac. You should be able to go straight across by now, but the path was still under construction through the open-cast site when we arrived and we were forced to turn right on the tarmac towards Stanley Crook into the teeth of a gale. We were reduced to the granny gears, but as we toiled around past the old school our spirits lifted when we realised that we were doing as well as a lad on a little motorbike. He never caught us. Perhaps he turned back!

You don't actually go into Billy Row, which some humorist with a spray can had altered to Billy Crow, but turn left onto the B6299 at the outskirts of the village.

Homeward from BILLY ROW

Follow the B6299 all the way to Willington, at ever increasing speed. A sporty Mitsubishi which passed us just prior to the steepest part of North Lane near Milkup Bank farm slowed to see how fast we were actually travelling, but drew away as we approached 80 kph (50 mph), obviously not wanting to become involved in the collection of our bits on the tight right-hander just after the ´30´ signs on the edge of Willington.

Turn left onto the main A690 through Willington, then left again onto the second railway path 800 m later, shortly after you pass the

Brancepeth Castle.

chippy. Just out of the town the track skirts one of the last heavy industries in the area, the Brancepeth Coke Works, then it is on through the fields to Brancepeth with its fine castle, where my Granny was in service many years ago. The path becomes single track and with the wind behind us we really flew, especially along the elevated section which skirts the village.

When you reach Brandon the track suddenly leaves the bed of the railway, weaves through young trees, then disappears at the edge of the playing fields only to reappear beyond a less than spectacular gate at the far side. There are a couple of roads to cross, then you can see Broompark across the valley, but the sting in the tail awaits.

The magnificent old wooden viaduct that spanned the River Deerness is long gone, so there is a very steep descent, a little concrete bridge, and then a horrendous climb back to the picnic place. Will your pride keep you on the bike, or will you simply run out of steam? I've seen it done, but never managed to ride to the top myself!

Dave Luke approaching the Whinny Lane crossing – it looks flat and effortless, but it´s not. Route 17.

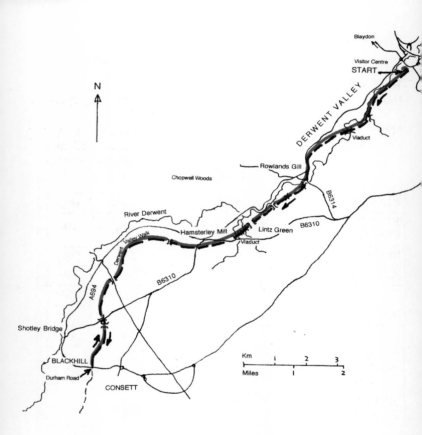

Blaydon

Visitor Centre
START

DERWENT VALLEY

Viaduct

Rowlands Gill

N

Chopwell Woods

B6314

River Derwent

Hamsterley Mill   Lintz Green   B6310

Derwent Valley Walk   Viaduct

A694   B6310

Shotley Bridge

BLACKHILL

Durham Road

CONSETT

Km   1   2   3
Miles   1   2

17. SWALWELL TO CONSETT

Grade: 4
Total distance: 34.5 km (21.44 miles)
High point: 213 m at the end of the route, Durham Road, Blackhill
Map: OS Landranger 88 Tyneside & Durham area
Facilities: Fish and chip shops at Rowlands Gill and Blackhill, pubs at Rowlands Gill, Broom Hill (above Ebchester) and Blackhill

PLOTTING PLAN	App.	Map ref.	Dep
START: Derwent Walk Visitor Centre, Swalwell	-	88/197619	SW
Rowlands Gill, A694, use footpath	NE	167588	SSE
Rowlands Gill, Stirling Lane	N	167582	SW
B6310, Hamsterley Mill	NE	142561	WSW
Medomsley Bank, B6310	ENE	133559	W
Broom Hill, Ebchester	NE	106547	SW
Blackhill, Consett. End of outward leg. Retrace outward leg to Swalwell	N	100518	N
FINISH: Derwent Walk Visitor Centre, Swalwell	SW	197619	-

If I want to get anyone into mountain biking, providing they have a reasonable fitness level, this is where I take them.

On the face of it a long railway ride has the potential to be boring, but this is not. The Derwent Valley is steep sided, you only need to step off the railway route to discover that, so consequently this is the easiest way to cycle to Consett, but it is still a fair pull. You start a mere 9 metres above sea level at the visitor centre behind Blaydon Rugby Club and finish the outward leg 203 metres (666 feet) higher at Blackhill, the average gradient being 1 in 66 for the last 12.2 km (7.5 miles). It is not unusual to see riders fading significantly in the latter stages.

I think I am correct in saying that this was the first "Railway Walk" in Durham, lying along the line of the Blaydon and Consett branch, built in 1864 by the North Eastern Railway company (NER), later to become the London & North Eastern Railway (LNER) and finally British Rail (BR). The original proposal for the line was made by the NER in 1859 as the Blaydon & Conside branch to oppose the Newcastle and Derwent Valley Railway (N&DVR) which would run along virtually the same course. The latter had the backing of the giant London and North Western Railway company (L&NWR) who were making great efforts to get a share of the extensive Tyneside coal trade. The House of Commons voted for the N&DVR proposal, but the decision was overturned by the House of Lords, in what turned out to be a landmark decision marking the last attempt by L&NWR to invade NER territory.

When you ride the line you will realise that the topography of the valley dictated the course of the railway, which in turn meant that stations were some distance from the villages it served as far as passenger traffic was concerned and made it most vulnerable to competition from the motor omnibuses of the 'Venture' and 'Northern' companies in the early part of the twentieth century. Apparently passenger totals sank from 665,000 in 1914 to 107,000 in 1934 with eventual discontinuation of passenger services in 1954. Freight continued until 1963, after which the track became heavily overgrown, but sterling work by the local authorities repaired damage to bridges, fences, the track itself and it was reopened as the Derwent Valley Walk and Country Park in 1972.

THE RIDE

The visitor centre is hidden behind Blaydon Rugby Club. Access to the railway is by either retracing 200 m down the approach road or cutting through the little park, which entails standing your bike on its back wheel to negotiate the barriers. If you retrace to the very start a signpost says "Rowlands Gill 3 miles", if you cut through the park you are greeted with "Rowlands Gill 5 km". Durham goes metric at last!

Straight away you see huge stone retaining walls on the left and get the impression that this railway was no mean undertaking. The terrain, as I have already mentioned, dictated the line of the track and also the building of some fine viaducts. Lockhaugh is the first, then beyond Rowlands Gill you ride over those of Lintz Green and Hamsterley Mill in very quick succession.

Use the shared facility footpath alongside the A694 in Rowlands Gill as far as the road junction with the B6314, which you follow down to the bridge over the River Derwent then cross the road into Stirling Lane and rejoin the line of the railway.

There are no major deviations from the trackbed between Rowlands Gill and Blackhill, but several road crossings where care must be exercised. The line becomes even more rural as you climb south-west towards Consett with a tremendous selection of both deciduous and coniferous trees, occasional extensive vistas across to Chopwell woods and the hamlets of eastern Tynedale across the border in Northumberland, and virtually aerial views of the gardens clinging to the steep sides of the valley.

This is one of the best all-year routes anywhere. I ride it an average of three or four times a year, enjoying the different attractions of all the seasons, and by the time you've pedalled up to Blackhill on a winter day the fish and chips are brilliant. You will find the chippy about 200 metres down Durham Road from the point where we turn around at the cemetery.

You will have seen the signs imploring cyclists to slow down on the stretch between Swalwell and Rowlands Gill on the outward leg, and perhaps thought them unnecessary. You'll soon find yourself in the highest gears on the way back. Take care, this is a multi-use facility.

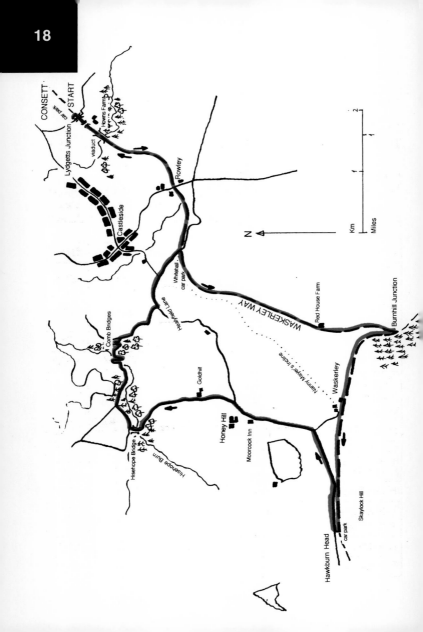

18. WASKERLEY AND MUGGLESWICK

Grade: 4

Total distance: 23.0 km (14.3 miles) Off-road constituent 15.0 km (9.3 miles)

High point: Hawkburn Head carpark, 400 m

Maps: OS Landrangers 87 Hexham, Haltwhistle & surrounding area, 88 Tyneside & Durham area

Facilities: Moorcock Inn, Honey Hill, full facilities in Consett

PLOTTING PLAN	App.	Map ref.	Dep.
START: Lydgetts Junction, near Howns Farm, Consett	-	88/100494	SW
Rowley, A68, care crossing main road	ENE	087479	SW
Whitehall carpark	ESE	077477	W
Burnhill Junction	NNE	87/064444	NNW
Hawkburn Head carpark, current end of Waskerley Way. Approach on railway, depart on main road	E	032454	E
Honey Hill	SSW	052469	NNE
Hisehope Bridge T-junction	SSW	049486	ENE
Comb Bridges	N	060487	NE
Healyfield Lane	NW	068481	ENE
Whitehall carpark, rejoin Waskerley Way	NW	88/077477	E
Rowley, A68, care	SW	087479	ENE
FINISH: Lydgetts Junction, Consett	SW	100494	-

This ride is essentially the same as the "Waskerley Way For Sprogs", but includes part of the amazing network of little roads near Muggleswick in the valley of the Hisehope Burn. They are very steeply down and equally as fierce uphill, very often damp, even in summer due to extensive tree cover, and occasionally liberally sprinkled with sand and stones when the gutters have burst their banks. When I rode the route in order to measure the distance there was an additional hazard in the shape of a dozen or so cows straying on the narrow descent to the first bridge. I don't know who got the biggest fright, although the beasts were quite demonstrative!

CONSETT to HAWKBURN HEAD

This outward leg lies entirely upon the old railway that constitutes the Waskerley Way. Start at the huge old slag hopper at Lydgetts Junction to the south-west of Consett, accessed from the A692 between Castleside and Consett. The picnic area and carpark are signposted from the main road, and once you reach the carpark, you will see the hopper perched on the elevated railway. Make your way up to it, turn right and ride south-west over the stunning Howns Farm viaduct, along the single track past Middle Heads farm and on to Rowley.

Despite there being the full track width available, most of the traffic, both pedestrian and bikers, have focused into a narrow central strip making virtually all the riding single track and rather interesting in places. This is particularly noticeable beyond Rowley Station, which doesn't exist anymore, unless you pay a visit to Beamish Museum where it has been rebuilt as one of the main exhibits. The bridge at Whitehall has vanished too, but take note of the road crossing – this is where you rejoin the outward route on the return leg.

Beyond Whitehall carpark the old line climbs steadily all the way to Red House farm, and if you look over to the right, the path of the original railway to Waskerley can still be seen, culminating in the steep Nanny Mayer's Incline. Trucks were assisted up this final grade by a stationary engine before the track that you ride was constructed. There is a sticky stretch in the cutting to the south of Red House, with an alternative path along the top of the embankment which is the obvious track in the winter months. Turn nor-nor-west when you reach Burnhill Junction.

This final stretch through what remains of Waskerley to Hawkburn Head can be fantastic in winter. Alan Moore and I once rode it on a still day in the middle of January when the whole countryside was white. The photographs gave the impression of snowfall, but there wasn't. There had been night after night of severe frost which built up to cover everything from grass and heather, which looked like minute Christmas trees, to the stone walls and fences, which looked as if they had been roughly painted. A fantastic scene.

When you reach Hawkburn Head picnic area, which is totally devoid of seats or benches or any form of protection, being stuck on the top of Skaylock Hill, turn right to the road, then right again for the tarmac interlude, and possible refreshment at the Moorcock Inn.

MOORCOCK INN to LYDGETT'S JUNCTION

The road undulates down past the Moorcock, then our route bears left at Honey Hill water treatment works, towards Muggleswick. There is a scruffy little signpost which is easily missed, but you'll know which road is ours by the width and lack of markings! There are some fancy poultry at Goldhill, if you are going slow enough to spot them, then the hill really winds up. John Hardisty used this as part of the final round of the national road race championships some years ago, but received many complaints amid the spate of breakages and retirements! You will be fine on the mountain bike!

When you get to the first T-junction, turn right, signpost "Castleside", same at the next junction, then down through the most intricate of the bends, up the far side and T-junction left when you can´t climb any further, at Healyfield Lane, the main road, still signposted "Castleside". J E Morris, in his "Companion into Durham" described this section "a bit of charming wooded dell on the little Hisehope Burn . . . Into this the road drops, and out of it climbs, by pitches of what seems almost perilous abruptness." That was in 1951. It hasn't changed! All that remains is to pedal round to Whitehall carpark, rejoin the Waskerley Way and enjoy the final couple of miles of off-road to Consett.

The Bolland team at Waskerley, Route 18.

Investigating fungi on Back Lane, the big climb out
of Lanchester, Route 19.

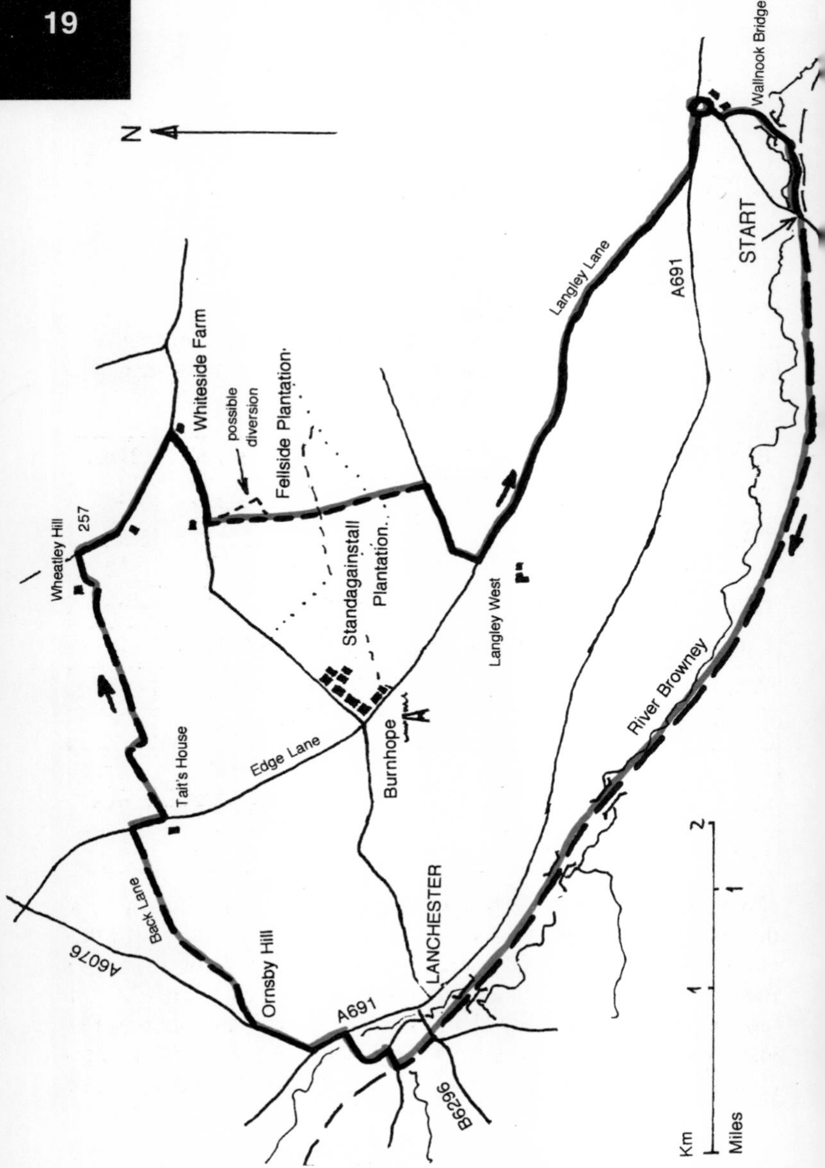

N

START

Wallnook Bridge

Langley Lane

A691

Whiteside Farm

possible diversion

Fellside Plantation.

Wheatley Hill 257

Standagainstall Plantation.

Langley West

Tait's House

Edge Lane

Burnhope

River Browney

Back Lane

Ornsby Hill

LANCHESTER

A6076

A691

B6296

Km

Miles

19. LANCHESTER HIGH LANDS

Grade: 5
Total distance: 19.0 km (11.8 miles)
High point: Wheatley Hill 257 m
Map: OS Landranger 88 Tyneside & Durham area
Facilities: Pubs in Lanchester and "The Centurion" near the finish in Langley Park

PLOTTING PLAN	App.	Map ref.	Dep.
START: Railway Walk carpark, Langley Park	-	88/215452	W
Lanchester, B6296	SE	165473	NE
Ornsby Hill (white road)	SSW	165484	NE
Unclassified road near Tait's House	SW	177491	S
Wheatley Hill	WSW	194494	SSE
Burnhope	E	196486	S
Langley West	NNE	194471	SE
Wallnook Bridge	N	221455	SW
FINISH: Langley Park	E	215452	-

Having ridden this route a debate developed with regard to which is the best way around. I used the author's veto to stick with the clockwise direction simply because I think every really good bike route should end with a wacky downhill. Langley Lane, albeit a tarmac public road got my vote, and I managed 71 kph (44 mph) in less than perfect conditions. The evidence in favour of an anti-clockwise tour is that the most difficult stretch of off-road, Back

Lane at Lanchester, would then be downhill and probably all ridable as a result, bolstered by the fast off-road downhill from Wheatley Hill. Why not do it my way first, and then in the opposite direction at a later date?

The debate was further fuelled by the original idea to start the ride at the Broompark picnic area, as with the Lanchester Valley ride, This would add 12.1 km (7.5 miles) of railway to the route, and if you're feeling fit there is no reason why not. One of the reasons behind this guide is to let you see what is available, then hopefully you will mix and match whatever suits you and devise your own rides.

Langley Park to Lanchester is a good warm up. The day we rode this it was foggy and cool in the Browney valley, but as soon as we started riding all this was forgotten as the enjoyment and interest of the ride took over. Another original idea had been to weave through the back streets of Lanchester to avoid the A691, but in all fairness the new road is wide and there is no problem. Whatever you choose you will end up on the A691 in time to turn right up Lanchester Bank on the A6076 towards Annfield Plain. This isn't a long slog because you fork right into Ornsby Hill after 360 metres, billed as a cul de sac on the nameplate, but as far as we are concerned a great invitation.

The old road from Ornsby Hill to Edge Lane – the unclassified road on the top of the ridge – is called Back Lane and has two halves. The first starts with asphalt up past the cottages then shrinks to a skinny bridleway interspersed with odd bricks and stones dislodged by horses. This has obviously been an important road in the past, reinforced by some amazing stone, but nowadays it is heavily overgrown making glasses essential and providing a test of strength and technical competence. Beyond a dip where a nascent stream rises, the way is better defined but stonier, steeper and more difficult. However, the final stretch is well used by tractors, then even becomes tarmac for 100 metres before you reach Edge Lane. If you ride it all the way you have my admiration!

Turn right then left after 170 metres onto what is obviously a restored opencast site road. There are no bridleway signs but the new substantial gates and barrier are significant markers, then you follow the wide track all the way to Wheatley Hill, the highest point on the route. Get a good gear and twiddle all the way to the top.

From the top of Wheatley Hill there is a right turn and flee down to Whiteside Farm where you turn right, toil up to the speed restriction signs for Burnhope, and turn left onto a bridleway which will take you virtually due south past Fellside Plantation then up through the optimistically named Standagainstall Plantation. There are plans to divert the bridleway down to the sewage works then back again onto the present line at the bottom of the hill, but this is no big deal, just follow the signs if it happens.

(There had been a tremendous crop of blackberries in Back Lane, then a fine mix of edible fungi in Standagainstall Plantation which brought the suggestion from Pam, my wife, that you could gather the ingredients for a three course meal if you followed this route at the right time of year. The soup starter could have been made from the shaggy ink cap mushrooms we saw at Langley Park.)

Of course there is always a penalty. The track up through Standagainstall Plantation is wet throughout the year, very wet in winter, but there is better going just off to the side. When you reach the road, turn right, then left above Langley West farm, over a small rise then into the long, long downhill. Don't forget, you've got 71 kph to beat!

All that remains is to merge with the A691, down to the new roundabout where you turn right towards Langley Park, first left down the quiet road to Wallnook Bridge and past the obvious temptations of "The Centurion" to the finish. Even the wife enjoyed it!

20

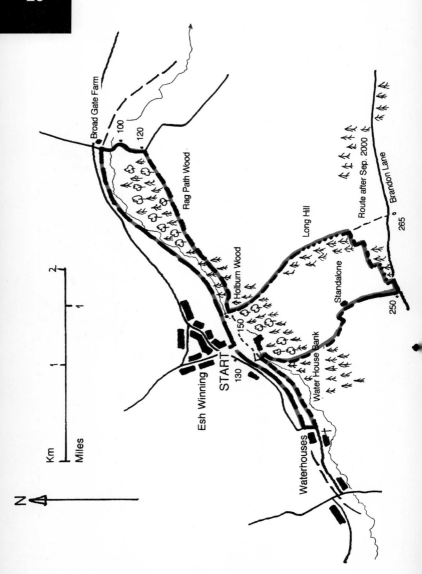

20. ESH WINNING WOODS

Grade: 5
Total distance: 12.1 km (7.5 miles)
High point: Brandon Lane, above Standalone farm, 255 m
Map: OS Landranger 88 Tyneside & Durham area
Facilities: Parking at the end of Station Avenue, opposite the Stag's Head, Esh Winning, next to the railway path. All manner of refreshment available in Esh Winning, nothing *en route*.

PLOTTING PLAN	App.	Map ref.	Dep.
START: Station Avenue, Esh Winning, join railway path	-	88/191416	SW
Buttons Place, Waterhouses, use bridleway parallel to railway path starting at the white chapel	ENE	183408	ENE
Bridleway bridge, Esh Winning	SW	190413	SSW
Water House Bank	NNW	191407	SSE
Standalone road end, Brandon Lane (just off map)	N	197399	E
(Diver. of bridleway – Sept. 2000 North Wood corner	*S*	*199401*	*NE*
Long Hill, end of Dolomite bridlepath	*SW*	*203405*	*NNW)*
Long Hill	SE	200411	NW
Holburn Wood crossroads. SP Rag Path Wood	SSE	195416	E
Rag Path Wood/unclass. tarmac road	SW	212424	N
Rejoin railway path, Broad Gate Farm bridge	S	212428	W
FINISH: Esh Winning	ENE	191416	-

On paper this ride might look rather contrived, using all the bridleways in a small area, but they are well worth riding. The grading might look a bit high for the distance too, but it was arrived at on the basis of technicality and the toughness of the climbs. You can always walk up the steepest bits, but you will need a fair degree of competence to ride the downhills, and an excellent degree of fitness to ride it all.

The November day I rode it – well nearly all of it! – there was a gale blowing, there was a constant threat of rain, at one point on Long Hill a constant shower of pine needles falling like orange snow, the tracks were covered in autumn leaves of every imaginable hue and it was terrific. If I had been fitter I would have gone around again just for the Hell of it!

THE RIDE

Hop onto the railway path at the bottom of Station Avenue and head south-west to Waterhouses. When you reach Buttons Place turn left down the main street to the old white chapel at the bottom, which has evolved into a garage, left again into a lane which soon loses its asphalt and ride back towards Esh Winning on a wide bridleway that is invisible from the railway. In places it is only 100 metres away, but you can't see it. There is a fine example of what I would call pitmen's fencing along the enclosures, not two posts the same and a neat but varied selection of wire. It all adds to the charm.

Having warmed up on the flat you now hit the hills. Just before you reach the cottages there is a small wooden bridge, signposted "Bridleway", which is a test of accuracy and control on the bike. Cross it and turn right again onto a stony lane which skirts the bottom of the woods on Water House Bank. The climb starts gently enough but bites after a small crossroads where the bridleway is the lesser track that goes straight up the hill. You'll see that the track has been surfaced in the past, possibly when the drift mine high on the hill was operational, but now it can be greasy with the odd loose stone to complicate the issue just when you start to tire! Follow the track right to the edge of the wood then make for Standalone farm just over the crest of the hill, beyond a cluster of gates.

Pass the farmhouse, complying with the signs, then join the tarmac farm access road which will take you up to Brandon Lane, from where Penshaw monument can be seen. Turn left, then we want the first bridleway on the left to ride down past the woods on Long Hill all the way to Holburn Wood crossroads, but until September 2000 there is a diversion to get around the opencast mining. The bridleway is still the first on the left, but it crops up only 100 metres after you join Brandon Lane, at a wicket gate in the new dry-stone wall. The diverted bridleway hugs the very edge of the fields, right next to the forest fence. There are signs to keep you right, so play the game and don't cut the corners. When you come to two gates in a field boundary, take the one on the right, this gives access to a good firm bridleway that runs along to the coal yard, then left down the western side of the wood to a purpose-built Dolomite track which will take you through Long Hill wood to the original bridleway on the eastern side. Turn left on the single track and hug the eastern forest fence.

There is the most amazing selection of gates down Long Hill, with the hard-packed mud track wandering a fair bit from its prescribed line, and a final stony descent through Holburn Wood to the "crossroads", which in actual fact are a well-defined bridleway junction. The track straight ahead will take you to Holburn Bridge, and you can see the Start, so there's an escape option here, but for those wishing to continue the challenge, turn right along a good track signposted "Bridleway to Rag Path Wood".

Again the old track has been paved in the past, is well defined and an easy ride to begin with, but you find yourself taking lower and lower gears until the realisation hits you that this is a very tough climb. However, once at the top the rewards are great. The bridleway which hugs the edge of the fields is well surfaced, apart from a few muddy splash pools, and increasingly downhill the farther along you travel. Bear in mind this thoroughfare is also used by pedestrians and horses, but most of the time the view is good and the riding great.

The old bridleway from Waterhouse to Esh Winning
along the Deerness Valley.

Turn left down a wacky little hill when you reach the tarmac,
through a ford which is seldom wet, and up the deceiving little hill
past Broad Gate farm to the railway bridge where you turn left onto
the railway again and head back to Esh Winning. I wasn't looking
forward to the wind in my face all the way back, but it didn't
materialise until I was within sight of the Finish. I didn't understand
why, and can't explain it, but was delighted just the same. The higher
your skill and fitness level, the more you'll enjoy this one.

Breakage can occur at any time or place and often high on a cold, windy moor. Be prepared!

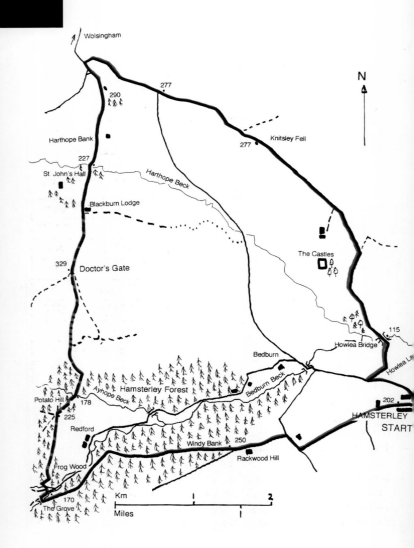

Wolsingham

N

277

290

Knitsley Fell

Harthope Bank

277

227

St. John's Hall

Harthope Beck

Blackburn Lodge

The Castles

329 Doctor's Gate

115

Howlea Bridge

Howlea La

Bedburn

Hamsterley Forest

Ayhope Beck

Bedburn Beck

Potato Hill

178

202

225

HAMSTERLEY
START

Redford

Windy Bank 250

Frog Wood

Rackwood Hill

170

The Grove

Km

Miles

1   2

21. DOCTOR'S GATE

Grade: 5
Total distance: 19.8 km (12.3 miles)
High Point: Doctor's Gate, 329 m
Map: OS Landranger 92 Barnard Castle & surrounding area
Facilities: Pub grub at the Cross Keys, Hamsterley village

PLOTTING PLAN	App.	Map ref.	Dep.
START: Hamsterley village green	-	92/115311	NNW
Howlea Bridge	S	111320	NW
Knitsley Fell	SE	095346	NW
Harthope Beck	N	073343	S
Doctor's Gate	NNE	070329	SSE
Potato Hill	NE	068310	S
The Grove	NE	066299	E
Windy Bank	W	090305	E
FINISH: Hamsterley	W	115311	-

My first six or seven visits to Hamsterley Forest were all in the navigator's seat of a highly-tuned rally car. My impressions were that it was a hairy place to enjoy oneself, underlined by one spectacular visit to a very wet ditch where we attempted to broadcast the contents over a wide area of County Durham, fortunately without injury or serious damage to the car. A second incident saw a lot of unintentional sideways motoring when a rear leaf spring broke at the end of a long straight, but the most spectacular was an end over end somewhere near Potato Hill, which seemed rather apt in retrospect. Hopefully your visit will be less dramatic!

The original plan for this ride included the excellent bridleways immediately to the north-east of Hamsterley village, joining Howlea Lane above The Castles, but unfortunately there is no right of way over the private bridge at map reference 123322, so that little bit has become the entertaining Hamsterley Back Lanes loop, and this tour starts with a high speed downhill to Howlea Bridge. A good compromise. Of course, if you feel super fit, there is no reason why you shouldn't add the Back Lanes to Doctor's Gate!

THE RIDE
Depart north-west from the village green T-junction, signpost "Bedburn, Hamsterley Forest". The road starts to drop steeply as soon as you round the slight left-hander, then after 700 m watch out for the junction on the right that will take you hurtling down to Howlea Bridge. Needless to say the climb up Howlea Lane, away from the bridge is every bit as sustained as you might expect, probably more. The navigation is easy, just stick with the tarmac and keep going up. I kept reminding myself that climbing on tarmac is easy, the rewards of downhilling on the loose would more than compensate, but it still hurt. However, there was a great sense of achievement on cresting the top of Knitsley Fell, and if you go at the right time of year there are excellent blackberries by the roadside.

When you reach the "Give Way" pause, then keep heading north-west for just over a kilometre (0.71 miles) where you turn sharp left, uphill, where the main road swings sharp right down to Wolsingham. There's no fingerpost, just a schematic "No Through Road" and a decrease in width. The map is slightly out in scale too which doesn't help, but start south-east with the skinny road, up the loose section which isn't shown on the map to rejoin the tarmac about 80 metres farther on. Then due south down a splendid hill to the Harthope Beck and up past St. John's Hall, which has got to be the only major house in the county which doesn't face south.

A gate marks the end of the tarmac at Blackburn Lodge, but the stony track to Doctor's Gate itself is less steep and eminently ridable. The Gate itself lies at the junction of stout moorland walls and a bewildering choice of several tracks, all heading south or thereabouts. The middle course is the Right of Way. This will take you through the old quarries then down on ever steepening and ever more broken track to the edge of Hamsterley Forest, where the bridleway is even steeper on the far side of the obvious gate.

There is an element of "do what you think is best" at the bottom of the hill, but basically you go straight ahead either through or over the Ayhope Beck then up Potato Hill. My legs just weren't working and I was forced to dismount. Loads of excuses, but I didn't ride it. Turn left at the forest crossroads at the top to skirt the fields of Redford. The loose road ends in a hairpin descent through Frog Wood to another ford, which can usually be taken flat out (famous last words!) and you'll find yourself popping out onto tarmac at The Grove.

Fork right for the toll road then hairpin left up over a steep bridge onto the long climb up Windy Bank to Rackwood Hill. It all sounds a bit intricate, but when you get there it sorts itself out. The final climb was more of a dull ache than a sting in the tail, and I was pleased to feast myself on the wild raspberries, a great excuse for getting off. Turn left at the T-junction and weave your way back to Hamsterley village.

I plan to return on a calm winter day, fancying the views across the moors will be at their best then, but if there's any wind at all, forget it.

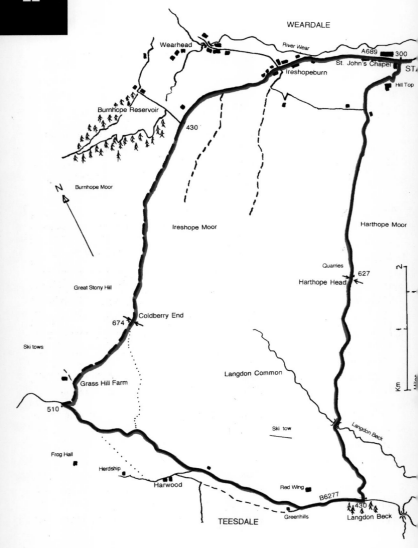

22

WEARDALE

Wearhead

River Wear

A689   300

St. John's Chapel   ST

Ireshopeburn   Hill Top

Burnhope Reservoir

430

N

Burnhope Moor

Ireshope Moor

Harthope Moor

Great Stony Hill

Quarries   627

Harthope Head

Coldberry End

674

Ski tows

Langdon Common

Grass Hill Farm

510

Ski tow

Langdon Beck

Frog Hall

Herdship

Red Wing

Harwood   B6277   430

Greenhills   Langdon Beck

TEESDALE

Km

Miles

22. HARTHOPE HEAD & COLDBERRY END

Grade: 6
Total distance: 23.3 km (14.5 miles)
High points: Harthope Head 627 m, Coldberry End 674 m
Map: OS Landranger 91 Appleby-in-Westmorland area, or 92 Barnard Castle & surrounding area
Facilities: Pubs in St. John's Chapel, Ireshopeburn and Langdon Beck (500 m off route). Apart from these this is a bleak ride!

PLOTTING PLAN	App.	Map ref.	Dep.
START: Farmers' Mart carpark, A689, St. John's Chapel	-	92/887379	W
Harthope Head, 627 m	NE	863350	SW
Bowes Close, B6277	SE	835324	NW
Grass Hill Farm, (derelict)	SSW	816353	ENE
Ireshope Moor, white road	SW	840376	NE
Ireshopeburn	W	866386	E
FINISH: St. John's Chapel	W	887379	-

When we stuck our heads into Michael Crompton's weaving shop at Ireshopeburn after a highly exciting but totally frozen descent from Coldberry End, he said "Well, you've done the classic", and that's what it is.

There is a large percentage of asphalt in this ride, but it is all good stuff. The major climb to Harthope Head is a killer, it just goes on and on. I don't know the average gradient but it just goes on and on, and, worse still, you can see what lies ahead all the way! You know exactly what you've got to do, and knowing doesn't help at all! The climb is 327 m (1073 ft.). There's another little pull from the bridge over the Langdon Beck, then a gentle but sustained push up the B6277 which regains another 80 m, and finally the loose track past Grass Hill Farm to Coldberry End which accounts for the last 164 m to the top at 674 m (2211 feet).

We passed a group of pseudo walkers who, not surprisingly, were spread all over the road as we pulled away from St. John's Chapel, but were immediately confronted by the devilishly steep little rise at Hill Top farm. Obviously we weren't going to get off in front of these people, but the situation was exacerbated by the fact that the whole road was covered in water ice. I chose a wandering but effective line which also used the full width, and made it. Jeff admitted his heart sank when he saw the hill, knew fine well I wouldn't get off, and was delighted to follow the leader. As soon as we were out of sight I stopped to take a photograph, the ideal excuse. When I checked the map later I noticed the Ordnance Survey had awarded the little blighter a single gradient arrow.

There's another single arrow climb soon after you get onto the hill proper, supposedly "1 in 7 to 1 in 5" – how come we were standing on the pedals in the granny gears. Either, we must be totally unfit or they've got it wrong. Probably a bit of both! It happens again before the old quarries at the top, but there is definitely a great sense of achievement as you crest the col . . . or is it relief?

For a change it wasn't windy. It usually is. I think it was in 1990, but it doesn't matter, that Alex Spence and I had met Adrian Gidney at St. John's when we were putting together the proper Coast to Coast route. We'd been exploring tracks on the north side of the River Wear, couldn't produce anything worth using and so decided to do this loop to bag a couple of OCD (L'Ordre des Cols Durs) claims. I foolishly suggested that we have our bait at the top! Not surprisingly I was last over the col, and then had great difficulty finding the other two who were lying in the only shelter, a large hollow. We dined flat, because every time you poked your head out of the hole you lost something. The meal degenerated into farce, bolstered by us giving Malcolm Williams, our regular companion, a right slagging for not turning out on such a nice day! The glee was topped out by the appearance above us of a perplexed motorist who had stopped to admire the view only to hear raucous laughter borne on the wind, but no-one in sight. It's a good job it wasn't Malcolm's solicitor!

Button up for the descent to Langdon Beck. Even on the best of summer days you will produce a high degree of wind chill due to your speed. On the day of the official ride I was forced to stop and place my map inside my coat to prevent chilling too much! There's a good view over the bridge across the Langdon Beck so you can usually straighten it out a bit, then a little uphill before the final twisty skoot down to the T-junction at the B6277.

The road north-west towards the Cumbrian border doesn't look at all steep but it wears you down. We had considered using the tracks through Greenhills, Herdship and Frog Hall but weren't too sure of their definitive status, so, coupled with the setting of a steady rhythm, stuck to the main road. There wasn't any traffic on it anyway, and you get great views across to the highest Pennines only 10 kilometres to the west.

Grass Hill Farm, which is merely a hillside hemmel[9] now, has become the traditional lunch spot. There is a complicated wall junction which can provide shelter from the wind, no matter from whence it is blowing. The turn through the gate was a mixture of water and ice, then the track mainly the latter. I asked Jeff to take his time so I could get a picture, so he did, and snapped his chain on his new Orange Clockwork. We walked up to the wall, dined with clean hands, and then fixed it.

Despite the ice much of the ride to Coldberry End was ridable, but once over the top the real fun started. The north-facing slope was ice, ice, and a bit more. Initially, on the rough ground down Great Stony Hill it was great, crunching in a major way, but when we reached the ancient tarmac it was great sheets of thick water ice across the entire width of the road. It must have been one of the slowest and most concentrated descents in recent times. You usually

---

[9] Hemmel – an open shed for housing cattle

Claire and David Logan climbing the loose road to Coldberry End.

get a sense of achievement from climbing big hills, this was the other way 'round. We had intended to make a loop across the Burnhope dam and down into Wearhead, but by this time were enjoying the high speed descent so much we missed the turn and thundered on down to Ireshopeburn, concluding that you would prefer to do the same. The sting in the tail came as we neared the village. Morning frost on the steep hill had melted, but it had now frozen again and a very delicate line and braking in the same vein was required. It was a good job nothing else needed the road.

Michael Crompton's weaving establishment is right on the junction with the A689. Well worth a look. Then it is straight along the main road, still virtually devoid of traffic on a winter Sunday afternoon, to St. John's Chapel. This ride is good at any time but has that extra spice in winter.

118

Intermittent snow and ice providing amusement across
Edmundbyers Common, Route 23.

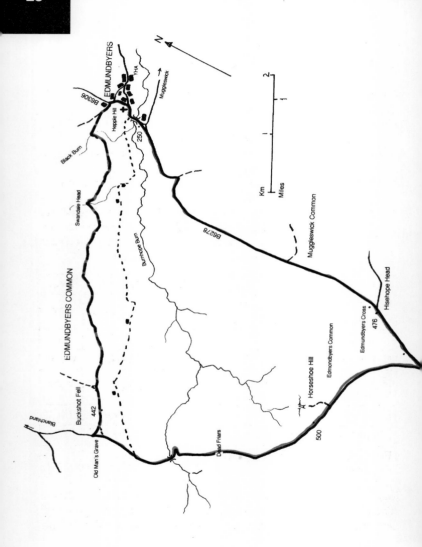

EDMUNDBYERS

B6306

YHA

Mugglewick

Heppie Hill

Black Burn

250

Swandale Head

Burnhope Burn

EDMUNDBYERS COMMON

Mugglewick Common

B6278

Hisehope Head

476

Edmundbyers Cross

Horseshoe Hill

Edmundbyers Common

Buckshot Fell

442

Blanchland

Old Man's Grave

Dead Friars

500

Km

Miles

N

2

23. EDMUNDBYERS COMMON

Grade:	5
Total distance:	20.3 km (12 .6 miles)
High points:	Hisehope Head, 476 m, Horseshoe Hill road, 500m, Buckshot Fell bridleway, 442 m
Map:	OS Landranger 87 Hexham, Haltwhistle & surrounding area
Facilities:	Punchbowl Inn and Youth Hostel in Edmundbyers. Nothing else
Note:	Avoid this route altogether between mid-April and the middle of June to allow the grouse to nest and hatch undisturbed. The main shooting season runs from 12th August until mid-September

PLOTTING PLAN	App.	Map ref.	Dep.
START: St. Edmund's church, Edmundbyers	-	87/015499	SW
Hisehope Head, B6278	N	004449	S
Horseshoe Hill	ESE	982446	WNW
Old Man's Grave, bridleway turnoff	SSE	963477	ENE
Swandale Head, usually ford	SSW	997496	ESE
Hepple Hill, Edmundbyers	W	014501	SE
FINISH: St. Edmund's church, Edmundbyers	N	015499	-

In the 17th century Edmundbyers became famous for its witches. There were tales of flying upon broomsticks to clandestine meetings and even dancing with the Devil. Famous among these was Jane

Frizzle of Crooked Oak, who, it is alleged, travelled by broomstick, casting evil spells on men, maidens and cattle, but you should be safe enough, since she lived over a mile away, just across the border into Northumberland! Rowan trees were planted in the gardens of farmhouses to protect them against evil spirits, especially the dead, but above all, as the sovereign protector of milk. St. Edmund's church, the starting point at the west end of the village, has several features to ward off witches and evil spirits – an "eye" window, gargoyles, a fine yew tree, the symbol of immortality even in pre-Christian times, and garlic in the churchyard, most noticeable in spring.

Travellers in the area always carried a crooked sixpence or gripped their thumb in the palm of their hand to safeguard them against evil. I can recall my granny, a Brancepeth woman, doing this as she walked along, but never questioned it until now, being more inclined to accept her philosophy: "If they pick me up in the dark, they'll put me down in the daylight!"

A churchyard pheasant reminded me of the bird life you will see on this route at any time of year. Mostly red grouse, telling you "back, back, back", but also a few pheasant, the odd curlew and some interesting Arctic visitors overwintering on the nearby reservoirs. These are well managed grouse moors. Please respect both the nesting and shooting activities.

THE RIDE

Follow the B6278, Stanhope road downhill from St. Edmund's, across the Burnhope Burn, past the Muggleswick road ends and up, ever up, onto Muggleswick Common. It is uphill for five kilometres, unrelenting, although some bits are easier than others. If the wind has any sort of southerly element to it, and any sort of strength, seriously consider the sense of attempting the route today!

The ruins of Edmundbyers Cross are allegedly to be found near Hisehope Head, 476 m, the summit of the climb, but the snow plough had apparently buried them, although a much finer marker, bearing a new bench mark, stands on the right, about a hundred metres before the turn towards Blanchland.

The signpost says "Blanchland 6 (miles)", but we turn off onto the bridleway at Old Man's Grave 6.3 kilometres across the moor. You may notice that this last stretch of tarmac lies across Edmondbyers Common, whilst the off-road phase lies over Edmundbyers Common. The 'o' and the 'u' are interchangeable. Beyond Dead Friars there is a vicious downhill hairpin, shown only as a 60 left on the Landranger. Beware, back off as soon as you see the warning sign.

Old Man's Grave isn't named on the Landranger, but the bridleway is shown and there is a Durham C C Bridleway post to mark the spot. A grouse road precedes the junction by about 100 metres. In all but the best weather you may need to walk the first 200 metres across the moor to join the grouse road, then the situation improves considerably. Just over 500 metres from the public road, bear right onto an entertaining little single track which will keep you on the line of the bridleway and deliver you to the appropriate gate. You now follow the grouse track again until it ends just over a kilometre farther on, where you wiggle through a gate in the fence onto lumpy single track that often doubles as the stream. Beyond the crest of the hill the track should lead you to a gate next to a wall. Again it is straight ahead.

There is more wet single track, leading after 1.5 km to the stream at Swandale Head, marked by a line of butts. Cross the stream and turn right onto a rough twin track, which will swing left maintaining height quite close to a high enclosure wall on your left. The track now gradually improves, swoops downhill, and culminates in the steep stony descent to Black Burn ford with Edmundbyers in sight. Care with the gate at the ford, it is secured by a stout metal spike driven into the ground. Lift, then open.

Follow the main farm track around to Hepple Hill, the junction with the B6306, where you simply dive right, down the hill, back to St. Edmund's.

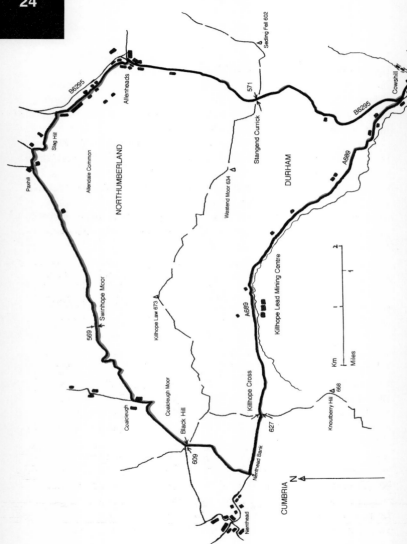

24. THREE COUNTIES LOOP

Grade:	8
Total distance:	23.4 km (14.6 miles) All asphalt
High points:	Stangend Currick, B6295, Northumberland border, 571, Swinhope Moor, 569, Black Hill, Cumbria border, 609, Killhope Cross, A689, Durham border, 627
Map:	OS Landranger 87 Hexham, Haltwhistle & surrounding area
Facilities:	Parking in Cowshill, signposted off north side of A689. Hemmel Coffee Shop and Café, Allenheads, highly recommended.

PLOTTING PLAN	App.	Map ref.	Dep.
START: Cowshill carpark, depart towards Alston, A689	-	87/856406	NNW
Stangend Currick, B6295, Northumberland border	SSE	853432	N
Allenheads. Use riverside road	SE	855459	NW
Swinhope Moor	ENE	824460	W
Black Hill, Cumbria border	NE	794444	S
Killhope Cross, A689, Durham border	W	799434	E
FINISH: Cowshill	NNW	856406	-

This is a bit of daftness to do on those winter days when it's actually too bad to be anywhere off-road, but you feel you should be out in the hills regardless! The basic route is all asphalt, but there are a couple of opportunities for rough stuff if you so desire. The idea

125

first came to me on one of those long winter nights gazing at the maps. I spotted this very high altitude corner of Durham abutting both Northumberland and Cumbria which had the potential for rich pickings in the way of OCD claims and the chance to visit three counties in a very short space of time.

L'Ordre des Cols Durs (OCD) is an organisation for folk who love riding high, and as you will have guessed from the name, started in France, where the Alps are the happy hunting ground for our Continental members. However, the eccentricity of it all obviously appeals to the English character and the English speaking section is one of the strongest. The basic idea is to take your bike over the highest passes or summits you can find and record the height as a "claim". I say take as opposed to ride because once you get into it things can tend to become a bit extreme – my highest claim being the Eisjochl or Pso. Gelato, 2895 m in the Sud Tyrol where I had to do a little rock climbing with the bike on my shoulder to surmount the col! For most of the members it is quite light hearted, but at the same time there have been some very serious routes done in pursuit of better and higher claims. For me the bagging of a new OCD claim has often been the catalyst needed to get out there on a day when it didn't look at all inviting, and the results have been some terrific days out, both in and out of the saddle.

The first time I did this route it was on one of those short winter days, 14 February to be exact, I didn't feel too good, needed some fresh air, so jumped into the car and within the hour was committed to a short but serious, snowbound route. Black skies followed me all the way around, but it never snowed and I ended up losing my headache and having one of the most memorable days awheel ever. Broke all the rules but got away with it. That particular version of the loop was shorter and illegal for bikes so I can't recommend it!

Of course there's nothing at all to stop you doing this in the summer, you'll find the Heritage Centre at Allenheads and the lead mining museum at Killhope open, places well worth a visit and a good excuse for a break before the next big hill. And these are big hills!

126

In 1995, inspired by OCD principles, I devised a route in these hills whereby heights equivalent to that of Mont Blanc, 4807 m (15770 feet) could be climbed in one day. I had a dress rehearsal but gave up about half way round after crunching through a lot of ice and carrying over far too much snow. However, I persuaded two far fitter friends, Emma Guy, better known as a demon downhiller, and Adrian Gidney, an endurance specialist, to give it a go for an article in Mountain Biking UK. Give it a go! They danced around in four hours two minutes, so how long will your total of 2376 m take?

The navigation could not be simpler. Up out of Cowshill towards Alston, bear right with the B6295 towards Allenheads, which is actually the main road. Over the top and down into Allenheads where you can cut the corner, using a steep little track signposted "Cafe" as you enter the village, wiggle along the bottom road by the river and then turn left at Slag Hill, signposted "Coalcleugh". Initially, this is a nasty climb but eases as it rises over Swinhope Moor, then there's an entertaining downhill *en route* to the Coalcleugh junction where you turn left for Black Hill and Cumbria. Again the initial hill is steep and often covered in ice in winter as I well recall.

I had been valley hopping one winter day and was coming in the opposite direction, downhill from Cumbria. Early frost and ice had melted and the roads had largely dried, but there were places where the low sun had never reached. It was approaching three o'clock and the temperature was plummeting. I had done about thirty miles both on and off-road, but was rushing back to the car and warmth. I had had enough, when, as I swept around the tight right-hander, I was confronted by sheet ice covering the full width of the road and a pair of Nenthead Hippies in a Citroen 2CV attempting to drive up the hill, but actually sliding sideways towards the Armco barrier. I slid into the barrier well before they did, managed to give a mighty kick come push off as I made contact, effected a speedway style passing manoeuvre past the Deux Cheveaux and somehow negotiated the tight left-hander which follows immediately. I recall the Hippies grinning as I flew past, and was convinced they were slowly descending despite their best efforts and a lot of wheelspin, then

Roadside leadmine entrance on the B6295 near Stangend Currick.

took to giggling as I hurtled onwards, imagining their account later in the day. "Crazy man, dope on the slope!"

The legitimate off-road option comes at the top of Black Hill. Turn right at the county boundary onto what is marked as a white road on the map and follow it all the way down into the back streets of Nenthead. The lane is entertaining and a bit rough in places, but the steepness of the Nenthead streets impresses me even more. The down side of this is the fact that you now have a longer climb up to Killhope Cross!

The soft (sensible) option is to go straight over the top past the Cumbria sign, down to the T-junction, then turn left onto the A689 and climb the upper reaches of Nenthead Bank to Killhope Cross. I am always impressed with the severity of what is alleged to be the second highest public road in England, and more than delighted to crest the summit. After that it is all downhill, well nearly all, to Cowshill.

'Novia Scotia' – a warning of what lies ahead, Route 25.

BALDERSDALE

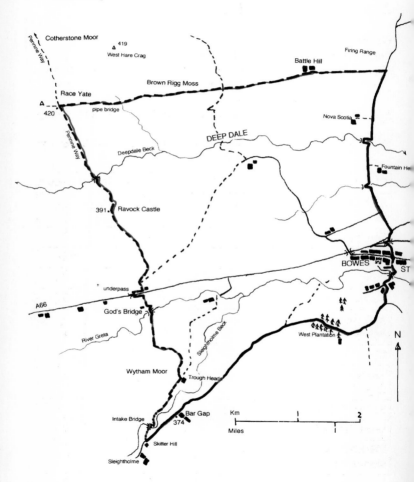

25. DEEP DALE SUMMITS

Grade: 9
Total distance: 22.9 km (14.2 miles)
High points: Race Yate, Cotherstone Moor, 420 m, Ravock Castle (ruin), 391 m, Bar Gap farm, Stainmore Forest, 374 m
Map: OS Landranger 92 Barnard Castle & surrounding area
Facilities: Pub and Club in Bowes, otherwise wild all the way!

PLOTTING PLAN	App.	Map Ref.	Dep.
START: Bowes & Gilmonby village hall carpark	-	93/996135	N
Fountain Head	S	991151	N
Battle Hill	ENE	980166	WSW
Race Yate, Cotherstone Moor	E	942160	SSE
Ravock Castle	NNW	951140	SE
A66 underpass (not on map - follow on site signs)	**N**	**954128**	**S**
God's Bridge, River Greta	N	957127	S
Trough Heads (follow white-tipped posts)	NW	961114	SW
Skitter Hill, near Sleightholme	NNE	956103	NE
West Plantation	WNW	986123	ESE
FINISH: Bowes & Gilmonby village hall	S	996135	-

In reality this is a dry weather route, otherwise it becomes a challenge out of all proportion to its length. A large proportion of the off-road section coincides with the Pennine Way, but you will be riding in the opposite direction to the bulk of walkers, so there should be few complaints of you silently sneaking up behind them and giving them a fright!

THE RIDE

The junction near the village hall in Bowes has sprouted a roundabout since the maps were last updated, one of the painted dot type. Head north from the carpark, through this roundabout, under the A66 trunk road, then left on the crest of the rise into a minor road signposted "Cotherstone". A sign says "Unsuitable for heavy goods vehicles" but the road remains quite wide, at least for the length of our usage, the advisory restrictions obviously pertaining to the bends and bridges over the burns you encounter before the Battle Hill turnoff. They aren't shown as much on the Landranger due to the scale, but you will find them quite entertaining in the flesh!

Turn left into the Battle Hill road, signposted both for the farm and as a bridleway. Skirt the farm on the south and keep heading west onto the moor above Deep Dale, which suggests a Yorkshire Dales connection both in name and appearance. This is limestone country, actually south of Teesdale, where many of the folk claim greater affinity with Yorkshire than County Durham, and within 5 km (3 miles) of the Cumbrian border, the accent of the shepherd I met *en route* confirmed this.

The good farm road past Battle Hill becomes grassy beyond a difficult gate, then more reedy and wet as you climb towards Race Yate. There is a rough bridge, just a couple of pipes and a load of rubble, 1.47 km (0.91 miles) before you reach Race Yate, a useful confirmation when you might begin to think that you are running out of road. Stick with the main track all the way to the wall. You can see a triangulation pillar away to the right atop West Hare Crag on Brown Rigg Moss, and may well have been accompanied by the sound of gunfire from the Battle Hill Range since leaving the tarmac.

You meet the Pennine Way at the gate at Race Yate, and turn left downhill. A fingerpost about 100 metres away to the right will give written confirmation if you need it. The accompanying stile provided me with somewhere dry for bait! You now follow the Pennine Way south all the way to the A66 and eventually to Sleightholme. In good visibility this is no problem at all. A new underpass through a reinforced galvanised tunnel removes any danger the A66 might have posed, then you cross the River Greta at the amazing limestone God's Bridge. The bridleways have been rerouted over Wytham Moor, but all you do is follow the white-tipped posts, then hug the walls and later the Sleightholme Beck to take you to Intake Bridge and Skitter Hill, then tarmac back to Bowes. Easy!

THE TRUTH

December 12, the A66 was open again between Scotch Corner and Penrith, having been closed for a couple of days last week. This route was expected to be well-defined tracks and bridleways, so there shouldn't be much of a problem, apart from being wet underfoot. Wrong!

The tarmac section up to Battle Hill road end was OK, but the farm before is called Nova Scotia, a harbinger of doom, or just a reminder of Canada in winter? The road to Battle Hill is rough tarmac, then stony through a couple of fields west of the farm. It started to become a bit of a toil immediately beyond the third field gate and I missed the alternative Pennine Way, which would have led past Goldsborough and down into Baldersdale. I think it must have been either very ill defined or covered in snow. However, on reflection it was just as well, since the extra rough mileage might have had dire results. Perhaps you might like to investigate it at a later date.

Moorland twin track with little in the way of easy going threatened to become single track after a couple of extra soft sections, but the Landrovers had created a ridable diversion. Then there was the rough bridge mentioned earlier and snow-filled ruts to point the way. The moorland road virtually follows the ridge and if there is any wind at all you will get it. The triangulation pillar provided a bit of reassurance as the light faded dramatically and black snow clouds threatened from the north-west. Then the last wall came into sight as I felt I should be eating something. The wall at Race Yate had a good pile of snow at either side and there was no protection, so I dined sitting on the Pennine Way stile about 100 metres north of the gate – the only dry spot on Cotherstone Moor. The white-topped mini-table mountain of Shacklesborough, 3.5 km away to the west-north-west started to take on an eerie atomic look and I decide it was time to get out of there.

The next 1.3 km (0.8 mile) downhill, with a height loss of some 85 m (279 ft) took 15 minutes! Skating through snow banks, over the 'bars a couple of times, plodging through sphagnum, leaping a couple of streams and generally making very hard work of the whole thing. The route grading leapt to 23!

Crossing the Deepdale Beck was effected via the bridge, a very narrow concrete beam with fortunately with a handrail on one side only, so you can carry the bike over your right shoulder and hold on with your left hand. Spectacular but safe. The Pennine Way continues south, across a new grouse road that isn't on the map yet, and up to and across an unnamed stream (at least as far as the Landranger is concerned). It then plods onwards towards Ravock Castle, which turned out to be nothing more than a pile of sandstone with two dressed blocks nestling among the debris. The visibility was decreasing by the minute and I was thankful for the occasional cairn. A walker had travelled in the opposite direction sometime in the previous day or two, but apart from myself there had been no other traffic in the last week. Some of the track was ridable, some of it very rocky, but much was too soft, too wet or plain too difficult. It should be infinitely better at the height of summer after the passage of a few hundred pairs of boots.

Eventually civilisation manifested itself in the shape of a wall, a post with the Pennine Way acorn for people travelling in the opposite direction, and then the increased roar from the A66. If you ever get lost up here just make for the traffic noise.

The new reinforced tunnel was a pleasant surprise, as was the downhill to God's Bridge – an amazing natural limestone arch through which the River Greta flows. This was something not to be missed. The shepherd arrived on his high-tech quad bike. As I ate the last sandwich, he showed me the best way up the hill onto Wytham Moor, not much of it ridable. The second phase across to Trough Heads has been diverted, but in normal conditions the white-tipped posts will be easy to follow. I followed the shepherd on his sweep search for strays.

When I reached Trough Heads I again followed the posts, jinked through the wall as directed to find the official Durham County Council bridleway diversion notification, then enjoyed the best and flattest riding of the day above the Sleightholme Burn. Aiming for Intake Bridge, the only one marked on the map, at 957106, I veered across to the lip of the valley after the next gate. In some places the scarp is so steep it has been fenced. Only about 30 metres before the first bank top fence there is a depression, a tiny corrie, this is the descent route! At first I ignored it and overshot, but this is it. Do not attempt to ride it in damp conditions! Need I say more?

Intake Bridge was even more hazardous, mossy wood with a veneer of frost – coupled to my muddy shoes, mine was not one of the more elegant crossings. It was with some relief that I reached the tarmac, but was forced to dismount and stand in the ploughed snow at the edge of the road to allow a Toyota pickup to pass, because I couldn't maintain a reasonable pace up the hill to Bar Gap. However, I got the legs working near the top of the hill and thoroughly enjoyed the six asphalt kilometres back to Bowes. The loop had taken 3 hours 58 minutes, a normal run will take half that time, or even less.

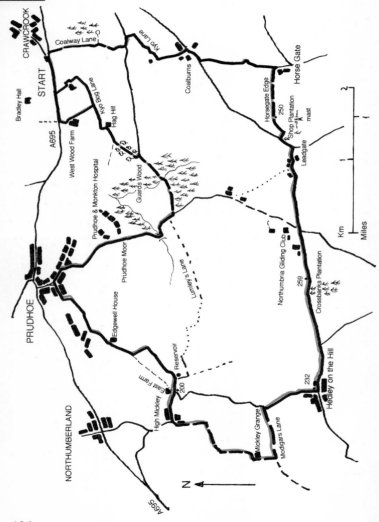

26. CRAWCROOK

Grade:	4
Total distance:	18.4 km (11.5 miles). Off-road 7.4 km (4.6 miles)
High points:	East Farm: 200 m, Hedley on the Hill: 232 m, Crossbanks Plantation: 259 m, Horsegate Edge: 250 m
Maps:	OS Landranger 88 Tyneside & Durham area (covers entire route)
Facilities:	Pub grub in Crawcrook and Coalburns

PLOTTING PLAN	App.	Map ref.	Dep.
START: Old A695 near Bradley Hall	-	128628	W
Guards Wood ford	NE	110612	WSW
Highfield Lane, Prudhoe	SE	096627	WSW
High Mickley	E	076611	S
Mickley Grange	N	071600	S
Hedley on the Hill	N	081592	E
Shop Plantation	SSW	115597	ESE
Horse Gate	W	125598	N
Coalway Lane	E	128618	N
FINISH: A695 Crawcrook	S	128628	-

The whole purpose of this route is to ride down Coalway Lane. Every good mountain bike route should finish with a downhill. This one has a cracker, steep, loose, technical, narrow and usually wet! Typical of mountain bikers, we ride a tortuous and sometimes difficult loop just to do the last kilometre in style. So what!

Actually this ride is the result of a lot of disappointments. The rights of way in the Crawcrook and Prudhoe area are a bit weird – lots of tracks that change status half way along; plus what lies on the ground is totally different to what one might expect in many places. However, you will see tempting opportunities as you ride around this route, so why not try them and see what happens. There were a surprising number of coal mines and you will find several spoil heaps scattered among the fields.

CRAWCROOK to HEDLEY ON THE HILL

Depart W along the A695 towards Prudhoe then left at the cattle crossing traffic lights and through Westwood Farm. This narrow road becomes the gloriously named Kyo Bog Lane when you turn right at the top. Then the first loose surface appears when you fork left after Hag Hill farm. It is actually a short but uncomfortable climb to the next junction, but once you turn right it is nicely downhill on a dirt road to Guards Wood and the fringes of the Prudhoe & Monkton Hospital grounds. It's a case of following your nose down what has been a paved road in the past, but is now well worn sandstone in many places, often covered with leaves and twigs. The ridable alternative, which is drawn on the sketchmap, is to turn right down to the bridge and follow Moor Lane.

The little ford at the bottom is no width at all but a bumpy challenge for your excursion into Northumberland. It should be ridable, but the hill on the far side is seldom dry enough to allow you to stay on the bike. The skinny tarmac road you eventually reach is Moor Lane and at the first attempt I turned right then immediately left through a gate which led onto a well defined grassy road. This connects with Lumley's Lane, a Road Used as a Public Path (RUPP) which weaves its way west to High Mickley. Unfortunately the road has seen very little use in recent years and at some points doesn't even exist on the ground any more, so despite the fact that I have good reason to believe it will be reclassified as a bridleway it was dumped. The ridable alternative is to follow Moor Lane up across Prudhoe Moor to the southern outskirts of the town then turn left at the signpost for High Mickley.

There are really good views over the Tyne Valley as you climb towards High Mickley, (if you have the fitness to look!). Then at a sharp left turn beyond Edgewell House Farm, the opportunity to go straight on onto another RUPP up the side of a field, is indicated by a blue bridleway arrow. If you choose this option act with due consideration at East Farm where there are stiles to be negotiated and even eight metres across the orchard lawn in front of the house! This section is delineated by "footpath" arrows just to add to the confusion. The alternative I chose was to stick with the tarmac, and the bonus is sparkling fresh water from a tap at the reservoir right at the top of the hill, where you would have come out if Lumley's Lane had worked. Reservoir is marked as such on the Landranger map but not on the Pathfinder.

Beyond the reservoir and East Farm, bear right, signposted "High Mickley", down the hill then straight on at the right-hander at the far end of the village onto a narrow track, signposted "Footpath which is actually a road, (the footpath runs alongside). It becomes a loose lonnen[8] weaving its way across the hill to Mickley Grange then south to another old road, Modigars Lane, where you turn left among a cluster of galvanised gates and "Private" signs to join the tarmac again for the climb to Hedley on the Hill.

HEDLEY ON THE HILL to COALWAY LANE

Turn east at Hedley on the Hill and although you climb steadily to Crossbanks Plantation, the highest point on the route, it seems easier than what has gone before. Northumbria Gliding Club is over on the left with the launching winch visible at the end of the field. As you crest the hill at the water tower you swap views down over the Tyne for the Derwent Valley. Then it's a shoot down through the hamlet of Leadgate, not to be confused with the place of the same name on the outskirts of Consett, and along to the left and then right turn onto Horsegate Edge near the transmission masts.

The old road across Horsegate Edge is gained through a seven-bar galvanised gate leading to a soft, rough, sunken track which is difficult in the extreme. However, it eases within 150 m and becomes

[8] Lonnen – lane

an enjoyable elevated ride, followed by a left turn onto a good tarmac descent to Coalburns (ignoring a right turn), where you turn left into a very narrow road, Kyo Lane, immediately after the pub. This takes you down to the last proper junction of the day, a tiny T-junction where you turn left between stout walls then right into Coalway Lane through what at times looks like a gravel heap, but then it's down, down, down in the climactic finish.

Initially the Lane is stony and hedge fringed, but as you increase in momentum the trees get bigger and the track smoother. The odds are that you'll miss the little turn off left with the true line of the Lane and shoot onto the huge forest turning circle, but it's no big deal, you'll not be the first! When you regain the correct, now very narrow and sunken track it becomes stony, with big stones at times. There is an enormous fallen tree that looks as if you may limbo it, but I have never succeeded. Then the track steepens again as you plunge towards Crawcrook. It is a real test of skill for all, and possibly bravery for many riders. All too soon you arrive back at the A695 and the finish. You could of course simply turn left along to West Wood farm, up along Kyo Bog Lane and do a little loop to see if you can make a better job of the final descent at the second attempt!

A major obstruction on Coalway Lane, the final descent to Crawcrook, Route 26.

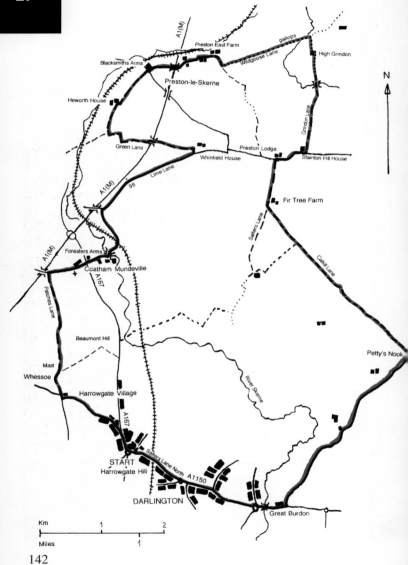

27

A1(M)

Preston East Farm

gallops

Widgoose Lane

High Grindon

Blacksmiths Arms

Preston-le-Skerne

Heworth House

Grindon Lane

Green Lane

Preston Lodge

Whinfield House

Preston Lodge

Stainton Hill House

A1(M)

98

Lime Lane

A1(M)

Fir Tree Farm

Foresters Arms

Salters Lane

Coatham Mundeville

A167

Cobwell Lane

Patches Lane

Beaumont Hill

Petty's Nook

Mast

Whessoe

Harrowgate Village

River Skerne

A167

START

Salters Lane North

Harrowgate Hill

A1150

DARLINGTON

Great Burdon

N

Km   1   2

Miles   1

27. DARLINGTON DEAD ENDS

Grade: 5
Total distance: 27.8 km (17.3 miles)
High point: Lime Lane, north of Brafferton, 98 m
Map: OS Landranger 93 Middlesbrough & Darlington
Facilities: Parking in Glebe Rd, Harrowgate Hill, Darlington, near school. All types refreshment in Darlington. Pub grub *en route* at Blacksmith's Arms, Preston-le-Skerne and Foresters Arms, Coatham Mundeville

PLOTTING PLAN	App.	Map ref.	Dep.
START: A1150, Salters Lane North, Harrowgate Hill	-	93/295173	ESE
Great Burdon	W	320165	N
Petty's Nook, turn left into Catkill Lane (bridleway)	SW	340190	NW
Fir Tree Farm, Salters Lane (again?)	SE	316215	N
Preston Lodge	S	317223	E
Stainton Hill House, turn left onto Grindon Lane	W	323224	N
High Grindon, near dism. railway	S	323244	WSW
Preston East Farm, Preston-le-Skerne	SE	240308	W
Green Lane, south of Heworth House	N	290228	E
Lime Lane, C class road	NE	295220	SW
Foresters Arms, A167, Coatham Mundeville. Care!	ENE	287206	WSW
Patches Lane, bridleway	NNW	281201	SSE
Whessoe, C class roads	NNW	283183	E
A167, Harrowgate Village	NW	293176	S
FINISH: Salters Lane roundabout A167/A1150	NNW	294173	-

By the time I had fought my way up the unused bridleway through High Grindon, or what remains of it, and then found that the bridleway alongside the dismantled railway line was actually alongside it on the south side of the fence and not superimposed upon the old trackbed, I was thinking "I can't send people along here", but then revised my thinking, considering that there is room in a guide of this size for a couple of really fringe rides, so reinstated the route as a challenge to the most determined of riders. You must be prepared to walk, push or carry the bike, and remove the vegetation from your chainwheels, gear mechanisms and possibly yourself from time to time! This is mad.

In addition to the madness you will need to conduct yourself in a most responsible manner. There are several gates to open and close on the bridleways, and in the region of High Grindon, obviously due to the fact that the bridleways see little use, many of them are overgrown. The farmer has left the statutory two metres alongside the edge of the fields, but the space is often highly vegetated, uneven and hard work. Regardless, do not walk or ride on the crops. The final real test comes in Green Lane, between Heworth House and Whinfield House farm. The road starts well, ancient tarmac, but once across the A1(M) you plunge into a section of overgrown single track where full protection is required, helmet, glasses, and tights. Added to this the riding is technical and by the year 2000 probably through a tunnel if the bushes are left to spread. After this you'll be ready for the Equatorial jungle, and all within sight of Darlington!

Dead ends will be proved wrong. You will pass many "No through road" signs along the route, which apply to motor vehicles of course, but it's great to demonstrate the lie.

THE RIDE

Depart south-east along the A1150, Salters Lane North, in the direction of Teesside. Unfortunately, pedestrian friendly islands have been provided at regular intervals which are quite hazardous for cyclists, many car drivers thinking they are a good place to squeeze past. Take care along this stretch. Turn left towards Sedgefield as soon as you pass through Great Burdon, and things improve.

The first bridleway, Catkill Lane starts at Petty's Nook, opposite Sadberge road end. Initially it looks as if it is going to be single track all the way, but then the track becomes broader, then soft and muddy, then takes to weaving about between the hedges after an amazing knackered gate which still closes on its spring. There are interjections of hardcore where muck heaps and field entrances occur, a blue bridleway arrow which has been subjected to intensive airgun practice and by the time you reach the junction with Salters Lane at Fir Tree Farm, you'll think you've had the full range of bridleway conditions.

Having started in Salters Lane North the inevitable question crosses the mind, are the two Salters Lanes related? With a bit imagination they can be connected, but how come the southern end has the northern suffix? Something to research in the long winter nights.

You turn right past Fir Tree Farm, right at Preston Lodge, then left through the farm yard at Stainton Hill House farm into Grindon Lane which will take you due north to the edge of the old railway. Initially Grindon Lane is wide and festooned with gates fastened by old harness chains, then beyond a new complex of fence and gates it becomes very soft and grassy and undergoes a total character change. There's an element of follow your nose at one point down the side of a small wood that is past its "harvest by" date, but you'll not get lost and soon traverse a small flat bridge flanked by tree trunks, a primitive but effective safety measure. This is where the difficulties start!

Immediately beyond the bridge the track disappears and the bridleway hugs the hedge on the left. The riding is difficult and the line somewhat vague, but by the time you reach the first gate you will be walking. The bridleway swaps sides of the hedge here. Go through the gate so the hedge is now on your right, and keep it that way up to High Grindon, where you will find that the old farmstead has disappeared and has been replaced by one huge barn and an implement storage yard.

There is a little mountaineering to be done to gain access to the yard, or you can sneak left around the barn. You end up in the same place. The gate onto the continuing bridleway will be found in the north-west corner of the yard, leading onto another stretch of the two metre statutory strip, with the fence on your right. It is soft and vegetated, but can be ridden, only because it is downhill. When you reach the old railway you'll find it has been converted to a gallop for race horses, and even if the right of way ran along it, would be unridable, but our bridleway turns sharp left and runs parallel to the railway fence along more soft, very vegetated ground. It is a walk, or even a fight at times! A single blue bridleway arrow shows the other bridleway that crosses the gallops, but there's nothing to point our way, the sole confirmation being a dismantled bridge lying piled at the side of a small burn which now needs to be jumped!

This is the worst bit, shown on the Pathfinder map as Wildgoose Lane. You will be forgiven for thoughts of Wild Goose Chase! I dined at the little, unused railway bridge after 800 metres, but will admit to sneaking onto the old trackbed when the gallops terminated about 200 metres later. Eventually you reach Preston East Farm and weave your way around to the "crossroads" at the Blacksmiths Arms, where, after suitable refreshment if required, you cross onto the well-surfaced farm road to Heworth House.

Pigs, excellent healthy big pigs, are usually found in the gated field on the approach to Heworth House. The farmer told me that the rings in their noses are to stop them digging up the countryside, and it works. The main paddock is a beautiful green field, unlike the conditions one often finds pigs in, and the pigs look excellent. Judge for yourselves.

South of Heworth House we turn left into Green Lane on ancient tarmac, cross the A1(M) again and then plunge into the overgrown challenge. Sloe berries abound, there are blackberries at the right time of year, and sundry bushes that will tug at your clothing, and you too if you are unprotected. The only consolation is that it is marginally easier on the bike than off! When you reach the Whinfield House access road turn right, then right again onto the C class road which is Lime Lane and the highest point on this low-level route, 98 m.

Friendly free-range pigs at Hewarth House Farm.

We now aim for Coatham Mundeville. Turn left before the bridge over the A1(M) and make your way to the crossroads by the Foresters Arms (another chance for refreshment) where with appropriate care you cross the A167, which used to be the A1 in my youth. Now head for Patches Lane, the final stretch of off-road. Ignore the last "No through road" and again turn left immediately before crossing the A1(M), at the entrance to Stanley Farm, but take the skinnier bridleway option. It would be wrong of me to reveal the final surprise – all I will say is go for it, you'll probably stay dry! Enjoy the final loose downhill past the mast on Beaumont Hill then follow the signs for Teesside when you get to the Whessoe district. This will take you back to the A167, then the A1150, and back to the start. It's a weird challenge, but in a strange sort of way quite rewarding.

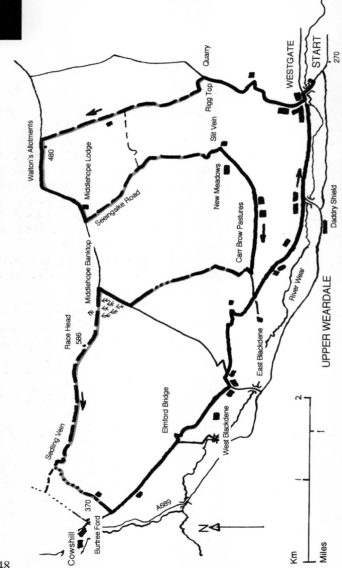

28. WESTGATE HORROR

Grade: 10
Total distance: 21.6 km (13.4 miles) Off-road 9.6 km (6.0 miles)
High points: Walton's Allotment road end 480m, Race Head 586m
Maps: The maps are a trifle difficult for this route, you need two regardless of your chosen scale. The Landrangers will suffice if used in conjunction with the sketch map. OS Landrangers 87 Hexham, Haltwhistle & surrounding area, 92 Barnard Castle & surrounding area. OS Outdoor Leisure 31 Teesdale, has most of the route, but the sketch map will suffice for the missing element.
Facilities: Very limited. Hare & Hounds, Westgate, pub grub at weekends and village shop/post office normal opening hours. Nothing *en route*.

PLOTTING PLAN	App.	Map ref.	Dep.
START: Westgate Community Hall	-	92/910379	NW
Rigg Top, turn left onto stony road	S	910393	NW
Walton's Allotment road end	SSE	87/903411	W
Seeingsike Road, Middlehope Lodge	ENE	893406	SE
Slit Vein, near New Meadows	NNW	92/901390	SW
Carr Brow Pastures	E	886387	N
Newhouse Moor	SE	87/882401	NE
Middlehope Banktop	SW	884405	W
Sedling Vein	SE	863410	SW
Burtree Ford	NE	857403	SE
West Blackdene	NW	92/870392	SE
East Blackdene	NW	886385	SE
FINISH: Westgate Community Hall	NW	910379	-

Make no mistake, this is a severe route, not particularly long but set in the tough countryside of Upper Weardale. The climbs are steep and unrelenting, the first rising from 270 to 480 m in 4 km (2. 5 miles), the second topping out at 586 m (1922 feet) on Race Head, only to be followed by one of the steepest and loosest descents anywhere in the Pennines. This is not for the inexperienced or faint hearted!

To be brutally honest the complete route took four attempts! The first, in the company of my long suffering mate Nick Eley on 8 August 1987 ended with a shortcut back to Allenheads on non-existent paths, which nearly killed us, the entire ride being in excess of 56 km (35 miles). The second, in May 1996 was abandoned in a freezing gale which swept across from Cross Fell. The third, on 3 September 1996 met a similar fate when Pam crashed very heavily on a rough section of Seeingsike Road and we were forced to freewheel back down to Weardale. Success was achieved alone two days later in heavy cloud and cold mist. It had become a challenge to simply complete it – perhaps a lot of fuss over nothing important, but it had to be done. Inasmuch as I love this countryside, you can't let it dictate the terms. Well, not very often!

There are two ways to do this ride. Either attack it and ride all the way if you are exceptionally fit, or accept that the hills are killers and be prepared to get off and walk when the going gets too hard. The latter has the benefit of allowing you to see some of the most beautiful wild flowers in the British Isles and many traces of the long-gone lead mining industry in a district that is officially designated an area of outstanding natural beauty.

WESTGATE to RACE HEAD

The Community Hall at Westgate used to be the railway station. It was one of five built as part of the Wear Valley Extension Railway which opened on 21 October 1895. This new line started at Stanhope and ran via Eastgate, Westgate and St. John's Chapel to Wearhead. The goods trains took limestone, fluorspar, timber and agricultural produce out of the Dale, and brought in coal, cattle feed, machinery and consumer items needed by the upper Dale community. During the 1950s the station and gardens won awards on four occasions, but sadly passenger services ceased in 1953 and the line was trimmed back to its present terminus at Eastgate in 1968.

Make your way back to the A689, turn left then right after 80 m at the signpost "Rookhope". The climb is horrendous, you could well be an expert on stone-loving lichens by the time you reach the turn-off onto the old stony road at Rigg Top! It is just beyond the quarry and big spoil heaps, and confirmed by a black "bottle" 50 m into the track.

There is actually a short downhill after you round the first corner, which may or may not please you, well knowing that you must regain the lost height on a rough road. Navigation is easy, simply follow the track all the way to the T-junction at the wild fellside called Walton's Allotment, marked by an old "Walls" van body. The height is now 480 m above sea level, so either button up or put your coat on for the descent to Middlehope Lodge. I clocked 68 kph, but I'm sure you'll do a lot better than that.

Beyond Middlehope Lodge turn left into Seeingsike Road, a rough track that becomes seriously bumpy. Watch what you are doing and try to maintain a reasonable speed, otherwise you will be caught out by one of the big holes. Another old road joins from the left after 1.2 km (0.75 mile) but keep right, and down towards the tarmac at Slit Vein, near New Meadows farm where you turn south-west, parallel to, but still well above the Wear valley.

An old, faded blue bridleway signpost points the way up the loose stony track to Newhouse Moor. A number of fine rowans or mountain ash line the lane, but if you ride this all the way you are good, very good. Just beyond the green gate there are a couple of heaps of stones, like BMX ramps, but they are not there for amusement, their purpose seems to be to impede the water which rushes down the track in times of heavy rain or thaw. Again the navigation is easy, simply follow the track between the walls until you break out onto open moor, and then keep close to the wall on the right.

When you reach tarmac again, turn right, then left at the top of the hill onto the loose track up through the trees, guided by a signpost for the "Lead Mining Trail". This takes you all the way to Race Head, the highest point on the route at 586 m, and a good place for a break. The views are great on a good day . . . they tell me!

RACE HEAD to WEARDALE

Once through the sheep pens at Race Head keep to the wall on the left. This will guide you down all the way to the Sedling Vein on the gloriously named Sedling Rake, but beware the "improved" stretches of bridleway – they are exceptionally bumpy at speed. My dictionary definition quotes rake as "to pass over violently and swiftly", and that is precisely what happens here. It is fast, bumpy, loose in places, then incredibly steep and loose in the final stages at Sedling Vein. Be sensible, if it looks too dangerous, which can easily happen in springtime due to the action of meltwater, get off before you become committed and walk/slide down!

There is also the small matter of finding the bridleway off to the left as you career downwards. It is without a signpost, difficult to find in the complex of old tracks and tramways, but cuts sharply back over a steep-sided burn then weaves across the fellside to join the higher Weardale road above Burtree Ford. If you miss it and end up in the bottom of the valley, which is very easily done, sneak through the old workings on the loose bumpy road as quickly and quietly as you can!

Even the asphalt finish is exciting. Take care at the hairpins at Elmford Bridge near Whitestones farm, then again in a steeper downhill version near East Blackdene where water and detritus can lie on the road at any time of the year, and finally on the last downhill to the valley bottom road at Daddry Shield Bridge. Apologies about the sting in the tail, the horrendous little climb from Newhouse to High Barnes, but it was all in a good cause!

The epitome of County Durham – moors and farmland, but always evidence of the industrial past.

More routes in The Lakes, Howgills & The Yorkshire Dales

JEREMY ASHCROFT

Due to the great demand from the author's first Mountain Bike Guide to the Lakes, Howgills and Yorkshire Dales, this second book has been compiled. Using the same format w superb two-colour maps and clear route descriptions, this second group of 36 routes provides the same variety of chalenge, from family rides to full-blown mountain adventures.

ISBN 0 948153-13-X   **£7.5**

North Wales

PETE BURSNALL

A long awaited guide. 26 excellent and varied routes, circli some of North Wales' most beautiful lakes, criss-crossing wide stretches of forest, and reaching the highest points. Great attention has been paid to access, and both local authorities and land-owners have been exaustively consulted Routes range from 10 to 60 km in length and cater for the family outing and the super-fit.

ISBN 0 948153-18-0   **£7.5**

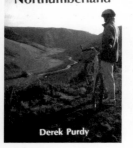

Northumberland

DEREK PURDY

32 well researched, totally legal routes throughout Northumberland, the best kept mountain biking secret in England. Bridleways, forest tracks, old drove-roads, ancier commercial routes, and neglected country roads.
Each route beautifully illustrated with black and white photos, two-colour maps, accompanied by technical terrai analysis and plotting plan, clearly written route description including a little local history and colour.
There are routes for all abilities.

ISBN 0 948153-16-4   **£7.5**

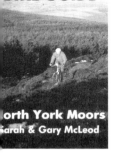

North York Moors

SARAH & GARY McLEOD

20 well-researched and legal routes over the open space of the North York Moors. Careful attention to conservation permeates the text with sites of potential erosion highlighted. All routes are clearly described and illustrated with two-colour maps and numerous photographs.
The guide caters well for family days but points out longer days through route linking for the young and fit.

ISBN 0 948153-30-X

£6.95

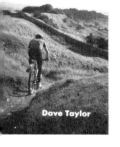

The Midlands

DAVE TAYLOR

This is the Mountain Bike Guide - family edition. The pages are packed with routes for fun days out or peaceful summer evenings in beautiful countryside.
But, Hammerheads, do not dismay! There are plenty of punishing climbs and the potential for some long, challenging days out.
Each of the 21 routes is illustrated with black and white photos and includes a two-colour sketch-map, local history etc.

ISBN 0 948153-29-6

£6.95

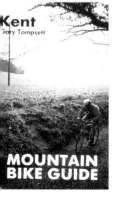

Kent

GARY TOMPSETT

21 well-researched circular routes throughout Kent - the garden of England. Discover this intricate county using the carefully drawn sketch-maps and clearly written route descriptions. Each route is accompanied by an unusual wealth of information on local history and geography, attractions and off route amenities and access rights. Black and white illustrations show the rich variety of landscapes visited. There are routes for all abilities, between 5 and 50 km, providing an essential guide for all off road cyclists. Beginners, families and expert riders will delight in the variety on offer. Just jump on your bike and go.

ISBN 0 94815-34-2

£6.95